Outside of a dog, a book is man's best friend.
Inside of a dog, it's too dark to read.
Groucho Marx

Purchase of this book was made
possible by a donation to the
Rochester Public Library Foundation from
Paul & Annette Godtland

MW00803787

BREITLING

Advertisement,
circa 1900

BENNO RICHTER

BREITLING

The History of a Great Brand of Watches 1884 to the Present

Revised 3rd Edition

Schiffer Publishing Ltd

Rochester Public Library

CHRONOGRAPHES
COMPTEURS
RATTRAPANTES

G. LEON BREITLING S.A.

MONTBRILLANT WATCH MY., LA CHAUX-DE-FONDS (SUISSE)

CATALOGUE SPÉCIAL POUR CHRONOGRAPHES - COMPTEURS BRACELETS

Catalog from 1920

Translated by Dr. Edward Force, Central Connecticut State University

This book was originally published under the title, Breitling *Die Geschichte einer Grofsen Uhrenmarke. 1884 bis heute* by Callwey Verlag, Munich.

Revised price guide: 2007
Copyright © 1995, 2000 & 2007 by Schiffer Publishing, Ltd.
Library of Congress Control Number: 2007923563

All rights reserved. No part of this work may be reproduced or used in any form or by any means—graphic, electronic, or mechanical, including photocopying or information storage and retrieval systems—without written permission from the publisher.
The scanning, uploading and distribution of this book or any part thereof via the Internet or via any other means without the permission of the publisher is illegal and punishable by law.
Please purchase only authorized editions and do not participate in or encourage the electronic piracy of copyrighted materials.
"Schiffer," "Schiffer Publishing Ltd. & Design," and the "Design of pen and ink well" are registered trademarks of Schiffer Publishing Ltd.

ISBN: 978-0-7643-2670-7
Printed in China
1 2 3 4

Published by Schiffer Publishing Ltd.
4880 Lower Valley Road
Atglen, PA 19310
Phone: (610) 593-1777; Fax: (610) 593-2002
E-mail: Info(a schifferbooks.com

For the largest selection of fine reference books on this and related subjects, please visit our web site at
www.schifferbooks.com
We are always looking for people to write books on new and related subjects. If you have an idea for a book please contact us at the above address.

This book may be purchased from the publisher.
Include $3.95 for shipping.
Please try your bookstore first.
You may write for a free catalog.

In Europe. Schiffer books are distributed by
Bushwood Books
6 Marksbury Ave.
Kew Gardens
Surrey TW9 4JF England
Phone: 44 (0) 20 8392-8585; Fax: 44 (0) 20 8392-9876
E-mail: info(a bushwoodbooks.co.uk
Website: www.bushwoodbooks.co.uk
Free postage in the U.K., Europe; air mail at cost.

Contents

Foreword

From its beginnings, Breitling has always looked to the future and will always remain so dedicated. At present, the future is broad in nature, offering more opportunities than either the present or past. We have set goals for ourselves and follow them diligently: to offer our customers a chronograph of the highest development using the newest technology. Developing this product involves a technology that is constantly changing. We must keep in step with these developments, being able to offer our customers the products and service that they have come to expect from Breitling in the past.

We take great pride in the development of the Breitling brand to date. With our chronographs, we have been able to maintain contact with our renowned past history and thus reclaim the stature that is associated with the Breitling name. When we acquired the Breitling brand from its founder's family in 1979, we knew only that part of the products had become legendary, especially those that were used by pilots all over the world.

In order to make the history of the Breitling brand better known to a growing group of admirers, Mr. Richter's total effort and tireless research gives well-deserved and noteworthy recognition to the creative powers of three generations of the Breitling family. We thank him most heartily.

With the knowledge of the Breitling firm gained herein, we hope that the admirer of chronographs and beautiful watches will appreciate this book. And we hope he will be able to value our work, whether in the realm of the traditional art of making complicated mechanical watches or in the art of modern electronics.

We hope you will enjoy reading this book.

E. Schneider   Grenchen, Spring 1992

Not long ago customers making purchases of new watches in jewelry stores and watch shops rejected the mechanical watch. They wanted something new, not something old-fashioned that had to be wound every day. There were very few people, even in the watchmaking business itself, who would have considered a rebirth of the popularity of the mechanical watch. A rebirth in the truest sense of the word did occur-- and to the manufacturers it gave justification to the fact that they had never completely given up production of the mechanical watch. Today the mechanical watch is more popular than ever. This is dramatized by a growing variety of publications about the mechanical watch as well as individual brands of watches. What the firms themselves have contributed to this rebirth, how they made further developments, and what became of them after all these years, is what this book is intended to portray of the Breitling firm. The known and the unknown about this brand are revealed in the following pages.

Heppendorf, August 1991
Benno Richter

Foreword to the Second Edition

The popular trend toward mechanical wristwatches continues now as it has before. Permanently rising sales prices in the most recent years are another indication in the interest as well. Among mechanical wristwatches, chronographs are definitely preferred by collectors now. Even if this reflects the trends of today's fashions, it is still clear that there always has been and always will be admirers of beautiful chronographs. The chronographs are unusual when compared to the other less complicated watches, and they have a certain sporty look. Because of this, established firms are reworking their existing models as they constantly bring new ones onto the market. In the offerings of the watch retailers the names of new firms appear again and again, with a growing number of new names in existence. Some time ago a race for technology among the manufacturers began, with more complications appearing in watches. Chronographs were made with the added complications of date and day indications as well as a full calendar, and, as a finishing touch, a sweep hand. One must wonder whether this new "packaging" is new or not. Even though chronographs with complications have existed for a long time, obviously the desire to be able to measure more and read more from the dial has inspired watchmakers to produce these more complicated watches. Therefore if the public's greater demand did not exist, we would have never created these wonderworks. For that reason we continue to hope that many sensible and functional ideas will find their way into this work of art called the watch.

Leimen, November 1994
B. Richter

The Breitling firm's emblems

Introduction

Regardless of what one chooses to collect, there is little doubt that if it is done passionately, the advocation will rob us of much time and trouble. For many people one of these collecting passions is clocks and watches. Well known watch and clock collectors include Henry VIII of England and his daughter Elizabeth I. In fact, this tradition of watch collecting has been maintained in the British royal family to the present day. Another great watch collector was the last king of Egypt, King Farouk. For all these well-known collectors, it was always mechanical timepieces that were collected. In these tiny mechanical instruments there is reflected the high degree of technology and ability of a time-honored profession. Whether the timepieces collected are tower clocks, regulators, pocket watches, observation watches, marine chronometers, wristwatches, or other types may not matter as much as the fact that they all have wheels that are turning and spring power that is turned into moving hands in remarkable ways, all for the purpose of indicating the time of day.

What does the collecting passion really consist of? For many, it is the constant search of the antique markets for a beautiful piece that could complete the collection. For others it may be going to auctions and being able to bid on and acquire a good item. For still others it is the detective-like search and subsequent exhilaration of finding offerings in newspapers and magazines or the special horological publications. Along another line, the watch could be sought by the collector for the purpose of monetary gain, as an object of speculation. With this comes the exchange of information, the "shop talk" among collectors and experts, as well as the permanent study of catalogs and other available literature on the subject. As long as people collect, this continual search will go on. Still another aspect of collecting can just be the pure joy in having the beauty or the brilliant technology of a watch in your hands. With a wristwatch, the harmony of case, dial and hands, along with the right band, can result in a small work of art that is well worth the efforts of collecting.

In the firm's early days, watches were usually marked on the underside of the dial, so that from outside it was not easy to see that the watch was made by Breitling. The signature at that time was "Montbrillant". Around 1930-32 the watches were signed with the "Breitling" script, which remained until the sixties. The Navitimer was an exception. Beginning in 1952 the "AOPA" emblem--the large wing with the letters on it, the big swallow--was used, since this watch was intended for pilots. Willy Breitling changed the "Breitling" signature in the sixties, since he was of the opinion that one could not easily read the name of Breitling in script form. He left the typical "B" initial on the dial, and the name could now be read in capital letters. Again it was only the Navitimer that had the two stylized airplanes on the dial as the firm's symbol. The firm's emblems changed more often in advertisements. The present Breitling firm has maintained the old tradition, and the present-day symbol consists of the "anchor" with the letter "B" in the center, plus the wings, to represent Breitling in the water, on land and in the air.

Since wristwatches are not very old, the hobby of collecting them is not either. Yet as young as this hobby of collecting wrist watches is, it is no less fascinating than the collecting of considerably older pocket watches. When one speaks of wristwatches, one thinks of great names, and behind every name is its own history. One of these great names is Breitling, and this book is intended to cover its history. The development of the firm can be divided into two eras: the first, from the firm's beginning in St. Imier in 1894 to its end as a family business in 1979; the second, covering the period from 1979 to the present under different leadership.

If the collector owns a Breitling wristwatch, all the features of his watch that are of importance will be covered in this book. But since it is almost impossible to assemble all the material on a period of more than a hundred years, about a firm that was constantly changing, this book cannot claim total completeness of information.

When one hears the name of Breitling today in connection with wristwatches, many first think of the classic Navitimer with its calculator and its various conversion tables on the dial. This was the watch which made Breitling famous far and wide. It was a sensation as soon as Willy Breitling put it on the market. However it was not only the Navitimer but also the chronograph watches for aircraft use that formed the basis of Breitling's success. This connection with flying with the Breitling firm has remained in existence to the present day.

The fact that the technically oriented watches have always held the highest rank in the Breitling firm cannot be overlooked when one looks at the firm's catalogs that were released throughout the firm's existence. In addition, there has been a series of less complicated wristwatches that should not be ignored.

The chronicles of the firm's history in this book, covering more than a hundred years of watch production with all its changes, begin in the year 1884. Based on the available information, this history will be chronicled with as many details as possible. These include the high and low points alike, as well as minor details, since often the small details make a history especially interesting. Along with the already mentioned Navitimer and the flight watches and chronographs that have spread the name of Breitling to all the world, Breitling has earned a reputation for precision and reliability. Whether a diver's watch or a timekeeper for an auto race, these watches have always provided reliable information. Breitling has been every bit as much at home in the "Admiral's Cup" sailing regatta as in bicycle or trotting races. From the firm's beginning to the present day, numerous watch models have conquered the market and created a unique image, and many of these watches, first purchased years ago, are still running as reliably today as when they were first made.

There are certainly problems of maintenance and repair of these mechanical watches. What is to be done if the watch is defective? Who can repair these old watches? How much longer will there be "old" watchmakers, who are being replaced by repairers who can only work on quartz watches. Who will supply the necessary parts, because when the firm was reorganized in 1979, there was not much left of the old machines and production materials. Most were sold or scrapped, and there are only small supplies of spare parts available today. Therefore having old watches repaired is a gamble, or maybe not possible at all. These and other questions persist. It would be welcome if there were greater numbers of mechanical watches today, which would mean that the new manufacturers could then efficiently provide service personnel.

Now let us turn to more than a century of Breitling history.

A note regarding the pricing herein. Some of the illustrations do not reveal whether the watch case is gold or steel, and unless indicated otherwise, the cases were assumed to be steel. Ordinarily the solid gold version is worth more than twice the steel one, a gold plated version (if the gold is not worn) is worth a bit more than steel.

Breitling—
The History
of a Great Watch
Manufacturer

The story of Breitling began on January 26, 1860, the day Leon Breitling, as a youth, first decided to learn about watches. Several years before that, his parents had moved from the Stuttgart, Germany area to the Swiss Jura to find work. During the summers they farmed the land and raised cattle, but during the long winter months it was necessary to work inside making clock and watch parts to supplement their limited income. These parts were later delivered to the watch manufacturers in the area. At this time out of a total population of 2.5 million people, some 40,000 people were working in the watch industry. Seventy five percent of these worked at home.

The parents of Leon Breitling settled in the town of Saint-Imier, which at that time consisted of only a few houses. Here Leon grew up and acquired the seeds of knowledge that were to lead to his later career. He was six years old when the International Red Cross was founded; twelve when the work on the St. Gathered Tunnel was begun. For Leon, hard work was his way of life from the beginning, and at an early age he was making mechanical components for watches from his home as a "cottage" worker. It was likely that complicated mechanical devices and timepieces attracted Leon even in his youth.

In 1884, Switzerland was in the depths of a recession, and many lost hope and emigrated overseas to begin anew. Also, Daimler and Maybach had just built their first motors, so an era of rapidly changing technology was dawning. Chugging automobiles and aircraft were first seen. The electric light was introduced, and countless other technical inventions were soon to follow. At this time there was also much happening in the Swiss Jura, in the Valleé de Joux. The ups and downs of the economy, especially in the watch industry, did not make starting a new business very easy. Nevertheless, at the age of twenty-four Leon Breitling finished his training as a watch-maker and opened a small studio in Saint-Imier to produce complicated mechanical devices and watches. He learned in a short time that it was necessary to specialize, to avoid being just one competing among many. This venture was successful, so a little later he founded a small watchmaking firm under the name of G. Leon Breitling, thus laying the cornerstone for a great brand of watches. From then on, the Breitling name was to quickly become well-known.

The first products made by Leon Breitling were timepieces of his own invention and construction: various complicated watches and chronographs as well as several special measuring instruments that were needed in the watchmaking industry.

He introduced his products at expositions and thus gained a series of prizes and certificates of honor.

Saint-Imier soon became too small for him, and Leon Breitling looked for more space. It was therefore natural to move to La Chaux-de-Fonds, where the majority of his suppliers were located. La Chaux-de-Fonds was and is a center of the watchmaking industry. In La Chaux-de-Fonds he bought land on the Rue Montbrillant and built a factory. In 1892 the firm moved to La Chaux-de-Fonds, and Leon changed the firm's name to "Leon G. Breitling S.A. Montbrillant Watch Manufactory."

In this process, his small studio had become a large watch factory with sixty employees.

Much of the work was already assigned to small family businesses and workers at home, for it was impossible to employ that many people in his own factory. To be able to sell his products in France, he opened a branch office in France, in Besancön, but after a short while that was closed, since direct deliveries to France became possible.

On August 11, 1914, Leon Breitling died. His son, Gaston Breitling, enthusiastically began his career in the business after having been trained as a watchmaker. Upon Leon's death, the entire responsibility for the development of what was now a considerable firm lay in Gaston's hands. Leon had blazed the trail, and now it was up to Gaston to continue through expansion. Having already seen a bit of the world, he was now in a position to take over the leadership of the factory. Leon had groomed his son from early on for leading this growing firm, and had shown him the possibilities that good advertising and promotion would bring. Gaston's intentions were to further perfect the chronograph, which was the firm's

Leon Breitling, the firm's founder.

specialty product and which represented the strongest portion of the firm's sales. From that time on, Gaston spent all his free time developing this new chronograph market. He designed a great variety of chronographs, each with its appropriate dial. Later he patented and marketed the Vitesse (*Speed*), a stopwatch with a 30-minute indicator and a center sweep hand. The first orders for the Vitesse came from police authorities, who used them to carry out the first measurements of road traffic speeds. So the Breitling firm contributed to catching the world's first speeders. Probably the most remarkable innovation was something absolutely new: a stopwatch that was worn on the arm by means of a band rather than one attached to a chain and carried in the pocket. This "wrist watch" had become a success because of its appeal as an accent to sportswear as well as its application in the technical aspects of industry. But most of all this new

Advertisement, circa 1920

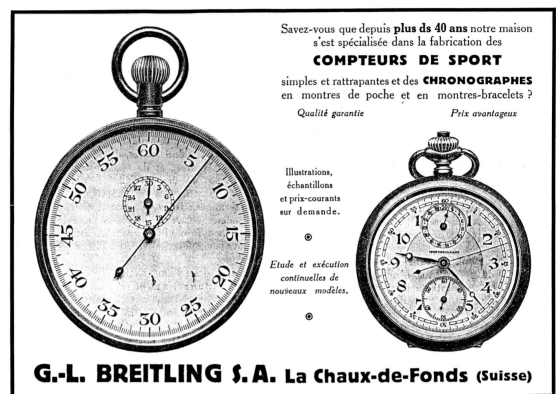

Savez-vous que depuis **plus ds 40 ans** notre maison
s'est spécialisée dans la fabrication des

COMPTEURS DE SPORT

simples et rattrapantes et des **CHRONOGRAPHES**
en montres de poche et en montres-bracelets ?

Qualité garantie   *Prix avantageux*

Illustrations,
échantillons
et prix-courants
sur demande.

◉

*Etude et exécution
continuelles de
nouveaux modèles.*

◉

G.-L. BREITLING S.A. La Chaux-de-Fonds (Suisse)

Advertisement, circa 1900

FIRST

compare quality and prices of

BREITLING TIMERS

and then, do what your own interest tells you to, that is to
say *place your next order with us !* Remember that *all our
timers are delivered with exchange materials in !*

G. L. BREITLING S. A.

MONTBRILLANT WATCH MANUFACTORY
LA CHAUX-DE-FONDS   (Switzerland)

MANUFACTURERS OF CHRONOGRAPHS
AND TIMERS OF EVERY DESCRIPTION

innovation was interesting to the military, and various governments ordered this new timekeeping instrument. The term "timing" became a new word, and Breitling was ranked among those who manufactured the finest timing watches. During the first years when these watches were made, there were usually no brand names on the dials, although some were identified with the names "Montbrillant", "Koko" or "Vitesse." It was not until the end of the twenties that the name "Breitling" begin to appear on the dials. Later, during the early thirties, definite serial numbers were used.

The political and commercial confusion of the First World War years did not leave the Breitling firm unscarred. When the European markets closed, Gaston Breitling had to search for new markets. This quarter century old firm would not give up under pressure and the crisis was overcome, thanks mainly to the firm's good name and to Gaston Breitling, who traveled much, knew the watch markets of the world well, and thus was able to assure the survival of the company by hard work. Because of increasing industrialization, it was evermore necessary to compare events with parcels of time: the revolutions of a motor per units of time; the speed with which something travels over a given distance. The Breitling firm designed time-event chronograph watches with special dials that could measure time-event situations. These ever-newer dial layouts with special scales and calculations greatly expanded Breitling's market. For example, for the church Breitling developed a counter called the "Unedeu" to count prayers. This was a counter in pocket-watch size with a three-digit indication operated by a push-button. The priest had this watch with him and thus always knew exactly how many of his flock had come to prayers.

Gaston Breitling

Willy Breitling

signed a large contract with the British Air Ministry to make flight chronographs for the planes of the Royal Air Force. From this time on, the Breitling firm would be associated with aircraft and aircraft navigation.

As time passed, more and more of the great aircraft manufacturers and airline companies took notice and signed contracts with Breitling. Pilots all over the world know the quality of the Breitling products and still swear by their chronographs today. The list of users' names included, but was not limited to, Douglas, KLM, BOAC, Lockheed, Air France, and United Air Lines.

The flight chronograph developed by Willy Breitling could not be excelled in precision and reliability, and this corresponded completely to the firm's theme of being simply the best!

Gaston Breitling died on July 30, 1927, and for several years the firm had no leadership. During this time, the day of the wristwatch for all levels of population had dawned; it was becoming a product for the masses. Once again Breitling had to specialize their products. At the beginning of the 1930s, they had forty chronograph models, and these numbers were to increase.

At the beginning of 1932, Willy Breitling, the only son, stepped into his father's footsteps and took over the firm. He had just finished his technical and commercial training and now wanted to lead the firm into the future according to new principles--with models and a long term goal. At this time, the chronograph for aircraft was developed by Breitling and was to carry the Breitling name all over the world. In 1939 Breitling

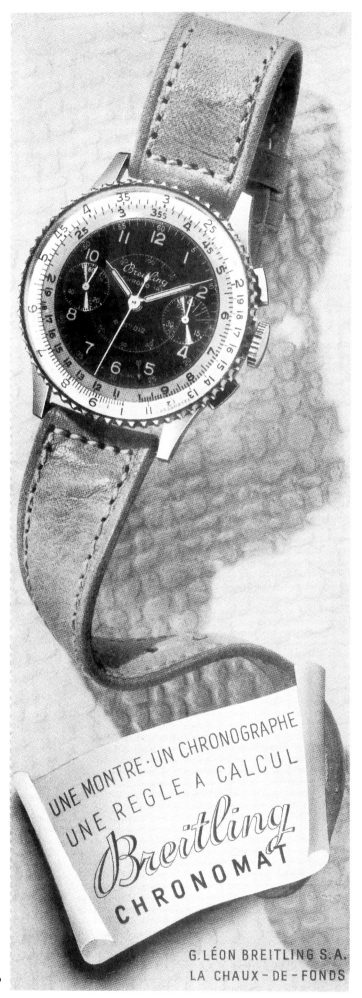

Breitling constantly took on new challenges in development and production. Engineers of the forties had lives dominated by measuring shorter amounts of time as well as percentages and quantities. For those who had to make a fast calculation on the spot but did not have a calculator at hand, Willy Breitling developed a chronograph that solved the problem. Along with the auxiliary dials, he added to the watch bezel a calculator that was turnable, making even complex calculations possible. This watch was called the Cronomat.

Once again, one sees how the firm's concept of producing technical products of the high-

Left: Chronomat advertisement, circa 1942 (left).
$1500-1800

From the 1936 catalog (right), lent by Auktionen Joseph, Top to bottom: $700-900, $500-600, $200-225.

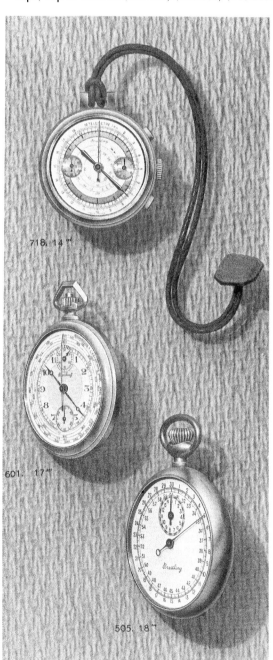

est quality has lived on through the firm's history. Rather than manufacture luxury watches and everyday watches, the Breitling firm instead strives for technical excellence, high precision products, and watches that help people in their effort to make technical progress.

Along with normal watches and chronographs, which have either snap-in or screwed-on back plates, waterproof watches have also found their place in the firm's offerings. Compression tests generally assured a waterproof seal up to two atmospheres, which is a water depth of twenty meters. Depths of 100 meters or more are obviously not yet required. The big catalog of 1946 included an array of about 250 different watches in six different areas, mainly chronographs. Through these developments, new generally applicable standards in terms of quality and reliability could be set.

In 1944 the Breitling firm celebrated its fiftieth anniversary. At that time Breitling released a publication which gave the history of the firm, including photos and remarks from various authors, including a great many customers.

The 1936 catalog, with various chronographs, lent by Auktionen Joseph, Left, $1400-1500 ea.; Center, $1400-1800 Ea.; Right, $1500-1800 ea.

Breitling

ALL TYPES OF
WATCHES AND
CHRONOGRAPHS

DISTRIBUTOR
FOR AUSTRALIA
SEGAL & C°
Wingello House
Angel Place   SYDNEY

Model 178
CHRONOGRAPH
EXTRA-FLAT
2 pushers, 17 jewels

A Breitling advertisement from
Australia, circa 1950. $1500-1800;
$2000-2200

Breitling

SPRINT-MONTBRILLANT

Opposite page: From the
1932 catalog, lent by
Auktionen Joseph. Top left:
$400-500; Bottom left:
$450-600; Bottom Right:
$900-1000, $1200-1400.

Pages 20 to 23:
Stopwatches shown in the
1923 catalog. Page 20
Top row: $200-250, $200-
250; Center row: $200-250,
$200-250, $200-250;
Bottom row: $200-250,
$200-250, $250-300.

Page 21
Top row: $250-300, $200-
225, $200-225; Center row:
$175-200 ea.; Bottom row:
$175-200 ea.

Page 22
Top row: $200-250 ea.;
Center row: $200-250,
$200-250, $200-250;
Bottom row: $175-200,
$175-200, $400-450.

Page 23
Top row: $400-450 ea.;
Center: $200-250, Bottom
row: $300-350, $75-100,
$200-250.

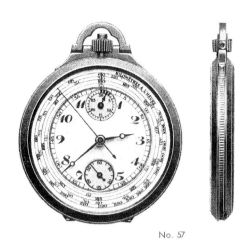

No. 57

CATALOGUE SPECIAL

POUR COMPTEURS SPORTS

Nos articles sont fabriqués avec mouvements ancre moderne, construits d'après les derniers perfectionnements techniques ; ils sont d'une qualité garantie en même temps que d'une grande précision.

Spécialisés depuis plus de 50 ans dans la fabrication du compteur sport, notre longue expérience nous met à même de lancer sur le marché des articles de confiance - répondant aux goûts et besoins de la clientèle - et d'étudier tous les genres rentrant dans le cadre de notre fabrication.

Tous nos articles sont couramment utilisés par les ingénieurs, mécaniciens, officiers, médecins, astronomes, sportsmen et, d'une façon générale, par toutes personnes tenant à faire des observations précises.

NOS NOUVEAUTÉS EN CHRONOGRAPHES :

No. 53

No. 54

No. 58

Mouvement ancre, très solide, construit d'après les derniers principes techniques. — Solides Anker-Werk," nach den neuesten Verfahren gebaut. — Strong lever movement, manufactured with the latest technical improvements

No. **1.** Compteur 1/5ème de 2de, petit compteur 30 minutes. — Stoppuhr 1/5tel Sekunde, Zähler 30 Minuten. — Timer 1/5th of second, recorder up to 30 minutes.

No. **3.** Même modèle que le No. 1, mais pendant ovale. — Gleiche Genre wie No. 1, aber ovaler Bügel. — Same style as No. 1, but oval bow.

No. **5.** Même modèle que No. 1, mais boîte verre plat, genre anglais. — Gleiche Genre wie No. 1, aber englische Form. — Same style as No. 1, but crystal shape.

No. **6.** Compteur 1/5ème de 2de, comme No. 1, mais compteur jusqu'à 60 minutes. — Stoppuhr 1/5tel Sekunde, wie No, 1, aber mit Zähler bis auf 60 minuten. — Timer 1/5th of second as No 1, but recorder up to 60 minutes.

No. **7-100.** Même article que No. 7, mais dont la grande trotteuse fait un tour en 100 secondes. Same style has No. 7, but full revolution of the large hand within 100 seconds.

No. **7.** Compteur 1/5ème de 2de, petit compteur jusqu'à 30 minutes, départ et arrêt par le verrou, remise à 0 par la couronne, cadran 100 parties donnant ainsi la 100ème partie de la minute. — Stoppuhr 1/5tel Sekunde, Zähler 30 Minuten, Ingangsetzen und Anhalten mit Schieber, Nullstellung mittels der Krone, Zifferblatt in 100 Teilen. — Stop watch 1/5th of second, register up to 30 minutes, start and stop through the slider. Fly back to 0 through the crown, dial with 100 parts giving the 1/100th part of a minute.

No. **7.A.** Même article que le No. 7, mais cadran habituel 60 secondes, compteur 30 ou 45 minutes. Gleiche Genre wie No. 7, aber gewöhnliches Blatt 60 Sekunden, Zähler bis auf 30 o. 45 Minuten.

No. **9.** Même article que le No. 3, mais plus petit modèle, sans cuvette. — Gleiche Genre wie No. 3, aber kleiner, ohne Cuvette. — Same style as No. 3, but smaller, without cap. Especially required for the Far East.

No. **10.** Compteur FOOTBALL fonctionnant comme le No. 7, mais muni d'un bouton de sûreté à l'anneau, compteur 30 ou 45 minutes. — Fussball-Stopp-Uhr, gleicher Gebrauch wie No. 7, aber mit sicherheitsknopf am Bügel. — Football Timer, used as No. 7, with safety bow. Recorder up to 30 or 45 minutes.

No. **11.** Compteur nautique 5 minutes. Régulièrement utilisé dans les courses de régates; il indique le temps restant à courir - minutes et secondes - avant le départ. – Segel-Stopp-Uhr 5 Minuten, unentbehrlich in Segel-Rennen, zeigt, vor der Abfahrt die noch zu laufende Zeit. – YACHTING TIMER, used in all yachting races, gives the time to be run before starting.

No. **12.** Compteur tachymètre, base 200 ou 1000 mètres, détermine sans calcul la vitesse à l'heure-parcourue par un véhicule quelconque, si celui-ci a franchi en 52 secondes une distance de 1000 mètres (200 mètres) sa vitesse à l'heure sera de 68 kilomètres (13 1/2 kilomètres). – Stopp-Uhr mit Tachymeter-Blatt, dient dazu die Schnelligkeit per Stunde eines Fuhrwerkes anzugeben. Wenn zum Beispiele 52 Sekunden erforderlich sind um 1000 Meter durchzufahren (200 Meter) so ist die Schnelligkeit pro Stunde 68 Kilometer (13 1/2 Kilometer).

No. **17.** Timer 1/5th of second with tachymeterdial 1/4th of mile. It mentions without any calculation the speed per hour of a vehicule. Example : If 52 seconds are necessary to go through 1/4 of mile, the speed by hour is 17 miles. No. **17** A. Same style as No. 17, but with 1/10th of a second and the speed is then based on 1/8th of a mile.

No. **12** A. Compteur 1/5ème de 2de, cadran pulsomètre, avec base 20 ou 30 pulsations. L'opérateur met le compteur en marche au moment où il perçoit la première pulsation; quand il a compté 30 pulsations, il arrête le compteur; le chiffre en regard duquel se trouve arrêtée la grande aiguille indique le nombre de pulsations à la minute. – Stopp-Uhr mit Pulsometer-Blatt. – Timer with pulsometer dial. – Cet article peut aussi se livrer avec 1/10ème de seconde, base 15 pulsations. ce qui permet une observation plus rapide.

No. **12** B. Compteur 1/5 de 2de, cadran production. (Taylor System.) Basé sur la fabrication, la production d'une unité, il indique sans calcul la production possible par heure. – Stopp-Uhr 1/5tel mit Leistung per Stunde : wenn ein Arbeiter, zum Beispiel, 1 Stück in 15 Sekunden herstellt, so wird es ihm möglich sein 240 St. per Stunde zu machen. Timer with production dial, gives the production per hour, based on one piece's production.

No. **18.** Compteur 1/10 de 2de, petit compteur jusqu'à 15 minutes. – Stopp-Uhr 1/10tel Sekunde, recorder 15 minutes. – Timer 1/10th of second, recorder 15 minutes.

No. **18** A. Même article que No. 18, mais compteur jusqu'à 30 minutes. – Gleiche Genre wie No. 18, aber Zähler bis auf 30 Minuten. – Same style as No. 18, but recorder 30 minutes.

No. **19.** Compteur 1/50ème de 2de, petit compteur 3 minutes. – Stopp-Uhr 1/50tel Sekunde, Zähler bis auf 3 Minuten. – Timer 1/50th of second, recorder 3 minutes.

No. **20.** Compteur 1/100ème de 2de, petit compteur jusqu'à 84 secondes. – Stopp-Uhr 1/100tel Sekunde, Zähler bis auf 84 Sekunden. – Timer 1/100th of second, recorder up to 84 seconds.

No. **20** A. Compteur 1/100ème de 2de; dont la grande trotteuse fait un tour en une seconde. – Stopp-Uhr 1/100tel Sekunde, Umdrehung innerhalb einer Sekunde. – Timer 1/100th of second, one turn of the large hand within a second.

No. **21.** Compteur ¹/₂₀ème de seconde, petit compteur jusqu'à 7¹/₂ minutes: – Stopp-Uhr ¹/₂₀tel Sekunde, Zähler bis auf 7¹/₂ Minuten. – Timer ¹/₂₀th of second, recorder up to 7¹/₂ minutes.

No. **68.** Compteur ¹/₁₆ème de seconde, petit compteur jusqu'à 10 minutes. – Stopp-Uhr ¹/₁₆tel Sekunde, Zähler bis auf 10 Minuten. – Timer ¹/₁₆th of second, recorder up to 10 minutes, especially used in dog races.

No. **70.** Compteur ¹/₃₀ème de seconde, petit compteur jusqu'à 5 minutes. – Stopp-Uhr ¹/₃₀tel Sekunde, Zähler bis auf 5 Minuten. – Time ¹/₃₀th of second, recorder up to 5 minutes.

No. **69.** Compteur 22" ¹/₁₀₀ème de seconde, petit compteur jusqu'à 120 secondes. – 22" Stopp-Uhr ¹/₁₀tel Sekunde, Zähler bis auf 120 Sekunden. 22" Timer ¹/₁₀₀th of second, recorder up to 120 seconds.

No. **66.** Compteur 19", ¹/₅ème de seconde, tachymètre avec base 100, 200 et 300 mètres. Recommandé aux autorités de police pour contrôler la vitesse des autos. – Stopp-Uhr ¹/₅tel Sekunde mit Tachymeter-Blatt, Basis 100, 200 und 300 Meter. Von Polizisten besonders geschätzt.

No. **61.** Compteur ¹/₅ème de seconde, avec poussoir indépendant pour la remise à 0. Peut aussi se livrer au ¹/₁₀ème de 2de, avec ou sans division décimale. – Stopp-Uhr ¹/₅tel Sekunde mit seitlichem Drücker zur Nullstellung; wird auch mit ¹/₁₀tel Sekunde gemacht. – Timer ¹/₅th second, fly back to 0 through side button. Can also be delivered with ¹/₁₀th second.

No. **61** A. Même genre que No. 61, mais compteur 45 minutes et chiffres et aiguilles radium. Gleiche Genre wie No. 61, aber Zähler bis auf 45 Minuten und Radium Zahlen und Zeiger. – Same style as No. 61, but recorder up to 45 minutes and luminous dials and hands.

No. **18** B. Compteur ¹/₁₀ de seconde, même genre que No. 18, mais cadran double échelle. Stopp-Uhr ¹/₁₀tel Sekunde, wie No. 18, aber Blatt mit doppelter Skala. – Stop watch ¹/₁₀th second, same style as No. 18, but dial with double scale.

No. **75.** Compteur rattrapante 3 pendants, marche permanente. – Doppel-Zeiger Stopp-Uhr, permanenter Gang, System AWF 2. Von den deutschen Ingenieuren besonders empfohlen.

No. **22.** Compteur rattrapante 17 ou 19" marche permanente, ¹/₅ de seconde. – Doppel-Stopp-Uhr ¹/₅tel Sekunde mit fortwährendem Gang. – Split second timer ¹/₅th second, permanent motion.

No. **22** A. Même genre que No. 22, mais ¹/₁₀ de seconde. – Gleiche Genre wie No. 22, aber ¹/₁₀tel Sekunde. – Same style as No. 22, but ¹/₁₀th second.

No. **23.** 17 ou 19" compteur rattrapante décimal, comme No. 22, mais cadran 100 parties. – Gleiche Genre wie No. 22, aber Blatt in 100 Teilen. – Same style as No. 22, but 100 parts' dial.

No. **23** A. Même article mais avec aiguille faisant un tour en 100 secondes. – Same style but full revolution of the large hand within 100 seconds.

No. **62.** Compteur industriel 28", solide boîte à vis, glace épaisse, cadrans avec gros chiffres facilement lisibles à distance. – Industrie Stopp-Uhr mit Schrauben-Gehäuse, dickem Glas und grösseren Zahlen auf dem Zifferblatt. – Industrial Timer 28" screw case, thick glass and bold dial.

No. **62** A. Même article que le No. 62, mais compteur jusqu'à 60 minutes. – Gleiche Genre wie No. 62, aber Zähler bis auf 60 Minuten. – Same Style as No 62, but recorder up to 60 minutes. – No. **62** B. Même genre que No. 62, mais remise indépendante à 0. – Gleiche Genre wie No. 62, aber mit seitlichem Drücker zur Nullstellung. – Same style as No 62, but side button to fly back to 0.

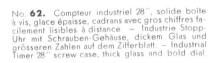

No. **63.** Compteur nautique 28", boîte à vis, même usage que No. 11. – Segel Stopp-Uhr 28" Schrauben-Gehäuse, wird wie No. 11 benutzt. – Yachting timer, screw case, same use as No. 11

No. **24.** Compteur d'unités, dit compte-moutons Nickel flache Beicht-Uhr. – Nickel sheep-counter – Construction solide, fonctionnement garanti, rapide remise à 0 par couronne spéciale

No. **64.** Compteur T S F, permettant moyennant conditions spéciales de déterminer la position exacte d'un navire. Demandez prospectus spécial. Special timer for taking bearings, screw case, is also made in a smaller model. Ask for special particulars

23

The 1928 catalog, lent by Auktionen Joseph. Top right: $250-300 ea.; Bottom left: top, $200-250, $225-250; Bottom right: $300-350 ea.

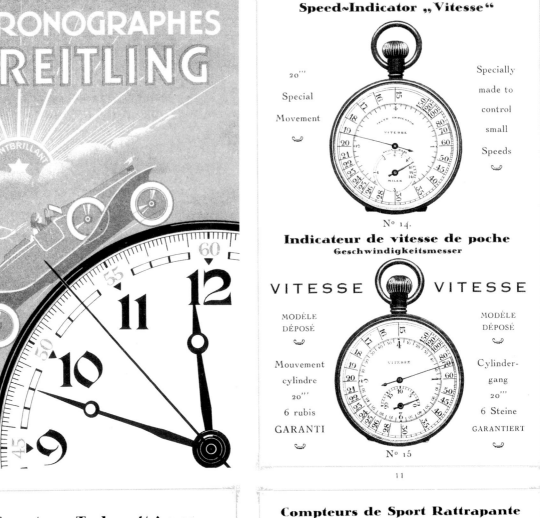

Speed~Indicator „Vitesse"

20'''   Specially
Special   made to
Movement   control
    small
    Speeds

Nº 14.

Indicateur de vitesse de poche
Geschwindigkeitsmesser

VITESSE   VITESSE

MODÈLE   MODÈLE
DÉPOSÉ   DÉPOSÉ

Mouvement   Cylinder-
cylindre   gang
20'''   20'''
6 rubis   6 Steine
GARANTI   GARANTIERT

Nº 15

11

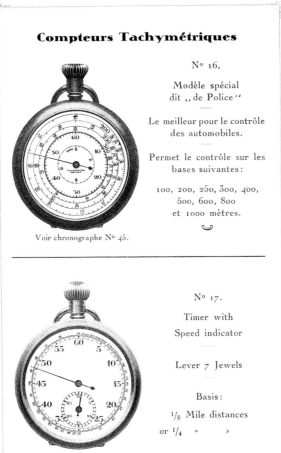

Compteurs Tachymétriques

Nº 16.

Modèle spécial
dit ,, de Police"

Le meilleur pour le contrôle
des automobiles.

Permet le contrôle sur les
bases suivantes :

100, 200, 250, 300, 400,
500, 600, 800
et 1000 mètres.

Voir chronographe Nº 45.

Nº 17.

Timer with

Speed indicator

Lever 7 Jewels

Basis :

1/8 Mile distances

or 1/4   »   »

PRICES WITHOUT COMPETITION

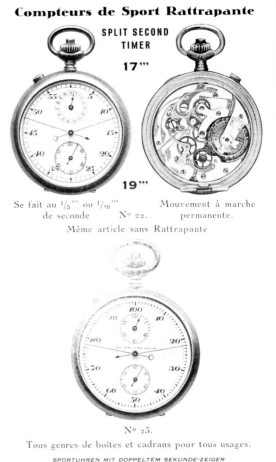

Compteurs de Sport Rattrapante

SPLIT SECOND
TIMER

17'''

19'''

Se fait au 1/5''' ou 1/10'''   Mouvement à marche
de seconde   Nº 22.   permanente.
Même article sans Rattrapante

Nº 23.

Tous genres de boîtes et cadrans pour tous usages.

SPORTUHREN MIT DOPPELTEM SEKUNDE-ZEIGER

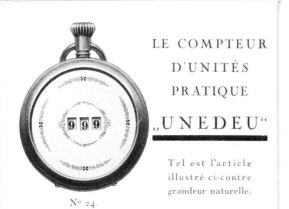

LE COMPTEUR
D'UNITÉS
PRATIQUE
„UNEDEU"

No 24.

Tel est l'article illustré ci-contre grandeur naturelle.

Il est employé avantageusement pour compter sans erreur ni fatigue la production des machines automatiques rapides ; il sert à l'élaboration des statistiques, à contrôler l'embarquement de têtes de bétail, moutons, par exemple, d'où son nom de **Compte-moutons**.

Il trouve son application pratique et avantageuse dans une foule de manifestations de la vie d'usine, sportive, etc.

Fabriqué en grande série par procédés mécaniques modernes, il vous offre tous les avantages : *Solidité, Précision, Bon marché*.

═══════

BEICHTZÄHLER

SEHR VORTEILHAFTE PREISE

SHEEPS COUNTER   CONTADOR DE CARNEROS

15

Mouvements
Chronographe~Compteur
„MONTBRILLANT"

No 27

No 28

Qualité B.
Ancre sp. bt. 15 rubis
n. mag.

Se fait aussi en 7 rubis
sp. plat.

Qualité A.
Ancre sp. bt. 18 rubis
rouges.
Bal. coupés, aciers de méca-
nismes chronog. anglés,
soignés sous tous les
rapports.

Ces mouvements d'une construction simple et solide, sont indéréglables ; le mécanisme construit mécaniquement d'après les meilleurs principes, bénéficie de notre grande expérience en la matière.

Les fonctions sont irréprochables et garanties.

La marche et le réglage de ces pièces sont l'objet de tous nos soins, car nous tenons fortement à contenter tout acheteur de nos montres.

═══════

UNE COMMANDE D'ESSAI NOUS PROCURE TOUJOURS
UN FIDÈLE CLIENT.

19

Chronographs for english market and colonies

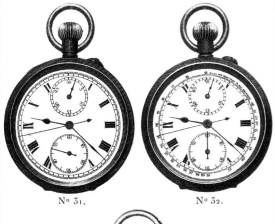

No 31.   No 32.

No 33.

SPLIT SECOND CHRONOGRAPH
WITH MINUTES RECORDER

21

Bracelet Chronographe

GRANDEUR
NATURELLE

No 37

Mouvement ancre sp. bt. 15 rubis. Qualité garantie.

Nous vous rendons particulièrement attentifs sur le système de *Poussoir du Chronographe* adopté dans ce bracelet. La place de ce poussoir, choisie très heureu-sement, facilite l'observation et rend l'emploi de ce bracelet très pratique.

──────

Wir machen Sie besonders auf das *Drückersystem des Chronographen*, der bei dieser Armbanduhr verwendet wird, aufmerksam. Die sehr gut gewählte Drückerstelle, erleichtert die Beobachtung und ermöglicht eine praktische Verwendung dieser Armbanduhr.

GRANDEUR
NATURELLE

No 38

Bracelet Chronographe Tachymètre

23

Top left: $75-100; Top right: $250-300, 300-350.; Bottom left: top, $350-400, 375-425, 500-550; bottom $350-400. Bottom right: $800-900, 850-950 ea.

25

During the twenties and thirties, many small firms were founded in the Swiss Jura that provided gears, hands and even watch cases with complete movements. These firms existed even in addition to the great raw movement producers of the time, such as Venus, Unitas, FEF, Felsa, and Landeron. Because of this diversity of labor within a limited market, Breitling's production was completely abandoned. This was because it was more costly for Breitling to create and maintain in-house manufacturing operations than to purchase the components elsewhere. Then in 1952 Willy Breitling decided to move the firm's headquarters to Geneva. In La Chaux-de-Fonds, where only production was carried on, the firm got by with limited personnel, and the production was limited to the finishing of movements purchased from other firms, adjustments, and setting the movement into the case. The firm was divided into Breitling et Montbrillant (in La Chaux-de-Fonds) where this production was done, and G. Leon Breitling S.A., Compagnie des Montres (in Geneva), which handled the administrative end. Delivery and distribution assuring easy availability to the customers have become increasingly important in modern marketing. For a long time, Breitling, like many other Swiss firms, have not produced their own movements, choosing instead to concentrate on their strength: the refinement of basic designs and designing special dials which set the Breitling watches apart from other brands. Two names have been very closely connected with the history of the Breitling firm. One is E. Stolz, who was in charge of administration and thus was the most important link between the firm and the retailers and customers. The other is M. Robert, the technical director in La Chaux-de-Fonds, who has a voice in the Breitling firm's new developments and also oversees production.

After the relocation, some thirty people were employed by Breitling in Geneva. Production went on at top speed, and sales were good. In the time that followed, Breitling was already thinking ahead, so that in 1952 another new chronograph, the "Navitimer", appeared. "Navitimer" is a word derived from "Navi", for the word "Navigation", plus the English word "Timer." It was truly a milestone and, as has been mentioned, for many people it was *the* Breitling watch or chronograph. Everyone knows and recognizes the Navitimer, the watch designed for flying enthusiasts, racing fans and sports people. With this instrument, all the necessary calculations for a rally or a flight could be made, so the Navitimer was more than just a chronograph, it was a complete navigational instrument on the wrist. It was universally usable in flying, and for that reason the first Navitimer bore the letters A.O.P.A., the initials of the "Aircraft Owners and Pilots Association", in the Breitling emblem. With all its special features, one might well think to ask whether the watch also showed the "normal" time. Naturally! If one wanted, it could even show a second time zone. One could start it anytime and use the secondary dial with 12 hour indication to show a second time zone. Ten years later, in 1962, Breitling put the Navitimer with 24-hour dial on the market. This watch bore the name "Cosmonaute." But whether Navitimer or Cosmonaute, with a Breitling one always had the exact time.

A Cosmonaute went on a trip into space on the wrist of Lt. Commander Scott Carpenter during the Mercury program. The watch had passed the extreme tests run by NASA on the ground, and now it had to prove itself in action, namely in flight under real conditions. The fact that a Breitling was chosen for this undertaking, as for so many others, did not happen by accident, for only good quality and reliability were so honored in the end. Once again, it was a great success for the Breitling brand.

Another watch in this series and from this era is the Co-Pilot, a chronograph with additional fifteen-minute indication, totalisator and rotating bezel, just as interesting for aviators as for rally drivers or sailors as a count-down counter at a boat race.

Many models and the names linked with them had already been registered by Breitling with the Swiss Patent Office in Bern. Thus many watch names were protected on a national, and still others on an international level. These include, for example, the Navitimer, Cosmonaute and Transocean. On the dial of the Chronomat with the calculator disc it is stated that this model is protected by patent law.

BUREAU FÉDÉRAL
DE LA PROPRIÉTÉ INTELLECTUELLE

Attestation

de l'enregistrement de la marque suisse N° **154683**

Le Bureau soussigné atteste qu'il a enregistré dans le registre suisse des marques, la marque dont la publication est reproduite ci-dessous :

N° 154683.   Date de dépôt: 22 janvier 1955, 8 h.
G. Léon Breitling S.A. Compagnie des Montres Breitling et Montbrillant (G. Léon Breitling Ltd. Breitling and Montbrillant Watch Manufactory), place du Molard 6, Genève (Suisse). — Marque de fabrique et de commerce.
Tous produits horlogers, montres, parties de montres, mouvements de montres, cadrans de montres, boîtes de montres, étuis de montres et articles d'emballage s'y rapportant.

Mandataire: René Mattioli, Dir. de l'Information horlogère suisse, La Chaux-de-Fonds

Date de la publication: Feuille Officielle Suisse du Commerce N° **48** du **26 FÉV. 1955**

BERNE, le **9 MARS 1955**

Bureau fédéral de la propriété intellectuelle
Le chef de section:

La protection résultant de l'enregistrement dure 20 ans. Elle est comptée : pour l'enregistrement d'une marque nouvelle, à partir du jour du dépôt de la marque; pour le renouvellement d'un enregistrement, à partir de la date indiquée dans la publication du renouvellement.

Le titulaire de la marque peut, en tout temps, pendant le délai de protection, faire **renouveler** l'enregistrement pour une période de même durée. Si le renouvellement n'est pas demandé dans les six mois à compter de l'échéance de la période de protection antérieure, l'enregistrement est radié et la marque ne peut être déposée que comme marque **nouvelle**.

CONFÉDÉRATION SUISSE

Attestation

de l'enregistrement de la marque suisse No **185738**

Le Bureau soussigné atteste qu'il a enregistré, au registre suisse des marques, la marque dont la publication est reproduite ci-dessous :

No 185738.   Date de dépôt: 14 avril 1961, 12 h.
G. Léon Breitling S.A. Compagnie des Montres Breitling et Montbrillant (G. Léon Breitling Ltd Breitling and Montbrillant Watch Manufactury), place du Molard 6, Genève. — Marque de fabrique et de commerce.
Tous produits horlogers, montres, mouvements de montres, boîtes de montres, cadrans de montres et parties de montres.

COSMONAUTE

Mandataire: René Mattioli, Dir. de l'Information horlogère suisse, La Chaux-de-Fonds

Date de la publication: Feuille officielle suisse du commerce No **127** du **3 JUIN 1961**

BERNE, le **-5 JUIN 1961**

Bureau fédéral de la propriété intellectuelle
Le chef de section:

L'enregistrement est valable pour une période de 20 ans, à compter de la date du dépôt de la marque. Il peut être **renouvelé** indéfiniment, à n'importe quel moment et chaque fois pour une nouvelle période de 20 ans, à compter de la date du renouvellement. Si le renouvellement n'est pas demandé dans les 6 mois qui suivent l'expiration de la période de 20 ans, l'enregistrement est radié; la marque peut être enregistrée à nouveau, mais avec perte du bénéfice résultant de l'enregistrement antérieur.

Trade-mark documents for the Navitimer and Cosmonaute

Various chronographs from the 1932 catalog. Top: from top to bottom, $700-800, $400-450, $200-250; Bottom right: $700-800 ea.

Page 29
Top row, left to right: $350-400, $375-425, $500-600, $300-400, $500-600, $550-650, $700-800, $700-800, $600-700; Center row, left to right: $500-600, $500-600, $550-600, $500-550, $500-600, $550-600, $450-500, $550-650; Bottom row, left to right: $350-450. $350-450. $300-400. $350-400. $350-400. $400-450. $400-450.

G. LÉON BREITLING S.A.
MONTBRILLANT WATCH MY.
LA CHAUX-DE-FONDS (SUISSE)

TÉLÉPHONE No 21.378
ADR. TÉLÉGR. : MONTBRILLANT

Breitling

MAISON FONDEE EN
ESTABLISHED
GEGRÜNDET 1884

Quelques références :

CHRONOMÉTRAGES OFFICIELS D'IMPORTANTES MANIFESTATIONS SPORTIVES

**TOUR DE SUISSE CYCLISTE 1936-37,
CHAMPIONNATS DU MONDE CYCLISTE
SUR ROUTE ET SUR PISTE 1936,
COURSES MILITAIRES DE SKI**
ETC. ETC.

TOUS LES APPAREILS DE CHRONOMÉTRAGE:

AVEC DÉCLANCHEMENT PAR PRESSION SUR TUYAU A EAU
AVEC SYSTÈME DE CELLULE PHOTO-ÉLECTRIQUE
AVEC FILM CINÉMATOGRAPHIQUE

1

10 1/2 '''

LE PLUS PETIT
CHRONOGRAPHE BRACELET
AVEC TOTALISATEUR
DE MINUTES
UN OU DEUX POUSSOIRS

THE SMALLEST WRIST
CHRONOGRAPH WITH
MINUTE'S RECORDER
ONE OR TWO PUSH-PIECES

DER KLEINSTE
ARMBANDCHRONOGRAPH
MIT MINUTENZÄHLER
EIN ODER ZWEI DRUCKER

3

4

12 '''

LE CHRONOGRAPHE **POPULAIRE**!
TRÈS ATTRAYANT!   BON MARCHÉ!

THE MOST **POPULAR** WRIST CHRONOGRAPH!
VERY ATTRACTIVE!   CHEAP!

DER **POPULÄR** - CHRONOGRAPH!
HOCH INTERESSANT!   BILLIG!

TOUS GENRES DE BOITES ET CADRANS
EVERY KINDS OF CASES AND DIALS
JEDE ART GEHÄUSE UND ZIFFERBLÄTTER

UN OU DEUX POUSSOIRS
ONE OR TWO PUSH-PIECES
EIN ODER ZWEI DRUCKER

DERNIER CRI   UP TO DATE CASES   STAINLESS STEEL   MODERNE GEHÄUSE

ACIER INOXYDABLE   ROSTFREIER STAHL

Breitling crée   *Breitling creates*

14 '''   **13 '''**   **13 '''**   ⊕ MODÈLES DÉPOSÉS

*P*OUR ELLE ET LUI

SOME SPECIALITIES
FOR LADIES TOO

16 ''' - 18 '''

SIE UND ER

No. 601 - 601F - 603
SANS CUVETTE
NO CAP
OHNE KÜVETTE

718
Châtelaine avec chaînette cuir

Spare parts for chrono-
graphs, 10.5 lignes

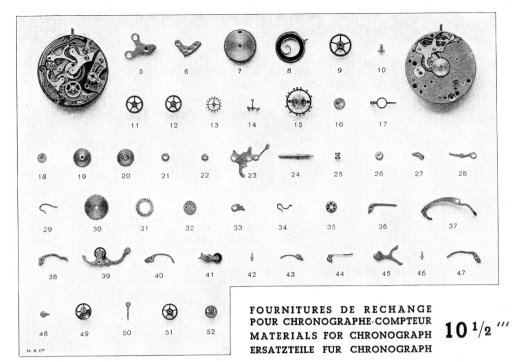

25

Spare parts for chrono-
graphs, 12 lignes

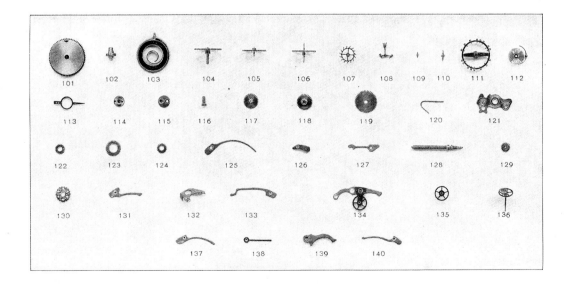

FOURNITURES POUR CHRONOGRAPHE SIMPLE
MATERIALS FOR SIMPLE CHRONOGRAPH
ERSATZTEILE FUR EINFACHER CHRONOGRAPH

12 '''

30

26

Chronographes 13-14-15 '''

1 à 2 poussoirs
1 and 2 push
1 oder 2 Drücker

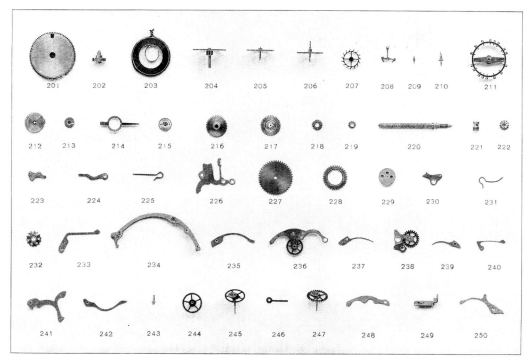

Spare parts for chronographs, 13-14-15 lignes

Pour obtenir la fourniture désirée, indiquer son numéro et la grandeur du calibre.
For obtaining the required material, please indicate the size of caliper and the number of material.
Bei Bestellung, erbitten wir um Angabe der Kalibergrösse und der Ersatzteilnumer.

Spare parts for chronographs, 17 lignes

FOURNITURES DE RECHANGE POUR CHRONOGRAPHE-COMPTEUR
MATERIALS FOR CHRONOGRAPH
ERSATZTEILE FUR CHRONOGRAPH　　　**17 ''' EC**

Spare parts for stop-watches, 18 lignes

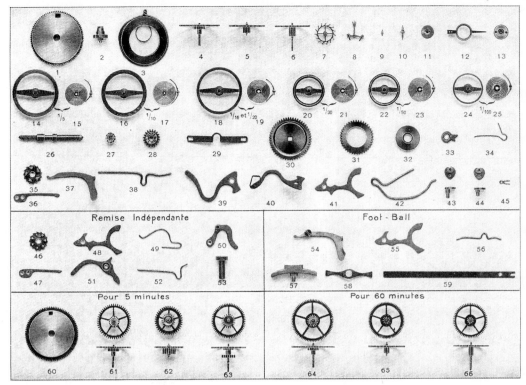

COMPTEUR DE SPORT
STOP WATCH
STOPPUHR

18'''

Spare parts for double-hand stopwatches

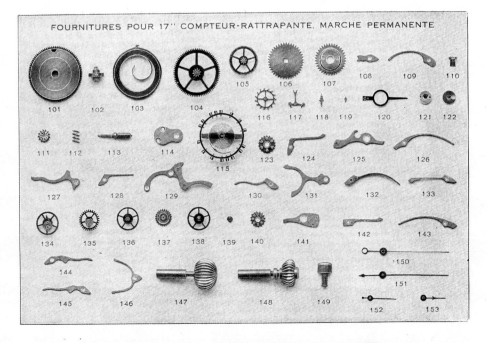

FOURNITURES DE RECHANGE POUR RATTRAPANTES
MATERIALS FOR SPLIT SECOND TIMERS
ERSATZTEILE FÜR DOPPELZEIGER-STOPPUHREN

Presentation of an award to Breitling for good advertising in the USA: G. Caspari (left), a McGraw-Hill representative (center), and Willy Breitling (right).

In the forties, Breitling conquered the American market. Here, in collaboration with Wakmann, the Breitling Watch Corporation of America was founded, appearing on the stock market in 1947. The stock capital amounted to $100,000, a thoroughly respectable sum. The Breitling Watch Corporation was a collaboration of Breitling with an American manufacturer, the Wakmann Watch Company Inc., which continued to distribute Breitling watches in the USA into the seventies. One still finds many watches that bear the name of Wakmann (or Wakmann/Breitling) on the dial and the case, or are signed by Breitling on the balance mount. These, then, are watches produced by Breitling, which were exported to America, the largest market.

The advertising Breitling did in America is worth study. Breitling advertisements in "Life International" magazine in 1956 always had a yellow background and stood out from other advertisements and resulted in a flood of inquiries, especially for the "Cardboard Watch." This was a "dry model" of the Chronomat, made to acquaint one with the operation of the watch. In addition, the 20th Century-Fox motion picture studio showed close-ups of the Navitimer in various films. In the film "Fathom", the actress Raquel Welch wears a Breitling Co-Pilot, and in "Operation Thunderball", James Bond wears a Breitling Top Time when in action. All of this made for good advertising for Breitling. In this field of advertising, there was only one name, one man for Breitling: Georges Caspari. From 1957 to 1986, almost thirty years, he was responsible for all of Breitling's advertising decisions. Successful advertising campaigns and market analyses, as well as his great knowledge of and interest in the watch industry, made Caspari invaluable. It was more than advertising that linked Willy Breitling and Georges Caspari; for over the years Caspari became one of Breitling's closest advisors, and he still thinks back fondly to those times.

In 1957 a reporter for "Time" magazine wrote the following about the Basel Model Fair: "The firm of Leon Breitling introduces a new stopwatch that is intended for engineers and technicians, and is equipped with a calculator as well as three hands for time and speed measurements. The price: about $100." This was the Navitimer, and Breitling could not ask for better advertising.

Because of more leisure time in our lives, there has been an increase in water sports. Breitling saw this trend and came out with a series of watches designed for water sport activity. The "Super Ocean" had its movement inserted from the top of the case, sealed with a reinforced glass, and was waterproof. A turning bezel for elapsed time calculations, and auxiliary dials, providing visible information about diving times or decompression times, were included.

Stock certificate of the Breitling Watch Corporation of America

★

Die vollständige Gebrauchsanweisung mit mehr als 20 verschiedenen Beispielen steht zu Ihrer Verfügung

ℬ BREITLING
GENÈVE
CHRONOMAT

Einige Beispiele:

Tachymeter

Auto

Ein Kraftwagen durchfährt 1 km in 40 Sekunden. Welches ist seine Geschwindigkeit? (in km/ Std.)
LÖSUNG : 1 (Streckenlänge) auf der äusseren Skala wird dem Merkzeichen S (Zeitmass) gegenübergestellt. 4 (40' Sekunden Fahrtdauer) deckt sich mit 9. Resultat : 90 km/Std.

Ski

Ein Skispringer macht einen Sprung von 55 Meter Länge und braucht dazu 3 2/5 Sekunden. Welches war die Stundengeschwindigkeit dieses Sprunges?
LÖSUNG : 55 (Sprunglänge) wird auf den Merkpunkt 1/5 eingestellt. (1/5 = Zeitmass) 3 2/5 Sekunden = 17 Fünftel. 17 und 58 fallen zusammen und ergeben ein Resultat von : 58,2 km/Std.

Radsport

Ein Radfahrer fährt mit einer Uebersetzung von 4,5 m. Welches ist seine Stundengeschwindigkeit?
LÖSUNG : 45 (Grösse der Uebersetzung) wird dem Merkzeichen S (Sekunden) gegenübergesetzt. Wenn nun für 10 Pedaldrehungen 16 Sekunden gebraucht wurden, ergibt sich bei der Zahl 16 das Resultat und zwar : 1 = eine Stundengeschwindigkeit von 10 km.

Pulsometer

Ein Arzt zählt 27 Pulsschläge in 24 Sekunden. Wieviel sind es in der Minute?
LÖSUNG : 27 (Pulsschläge) gegenüber dem Merkzeichen « Minutes ». Ablesen der Zahl bei 24 (Beobachtungsdauer). Resultat : 67 Pulsschläge in der Minute.

Telemeter

Ein Donnerschlag wird 4 Sekunden nach der Wahrnehmung des Blitzes vernommen. In welcher Distanz hat der Blitz eingeschlagen?
LÖSUNG : Merkpunkt « Telemeter » gegenüber 4 (4 Sekunden). Beim Punkt S wird abgelesen : 13,3 (,3 schätzungsweise). Durcheilte Distanz = 1 km 330 m.

Multiplikation

Der Multiplikant wird dem Multiplikator gegenübergestellt, d.h. vis-à-vis von « 1 » der einen oder anderen Skala kann das Resultat abgelesen werden. — Beispiel : 3 × 18 = 54.

Division

Die Division geht in umgekehrter Weise vor sich, indem die Zahl (1) der einen oder anderen Skala dem Dividenden gegenübergestellt wird, was eine ganze Reihe Divisionen hervorbringt, deren Resultate gegenüber dem Divisor abgelesen werden können, d. h. jeder gewählte Divisor deckt sich mit dem Resultat. — Beispiel :

$$54 : 18 = 3$$
$$54 : 45 = 1,2$$

Ankauf einer Ware à Fr. 6.— das kg brutto. Verpackungsverlust ist 10 %. Welches ist der Preis von 1 kg netto?
LÖSUNG : Gegenüberstellung von 6 (Franken) und (1) einer Skala und Ablesen des Resultates bei 9 (900 g), ergibt : Fr. 6,70 das kg netto.

Imprimé en Suisse

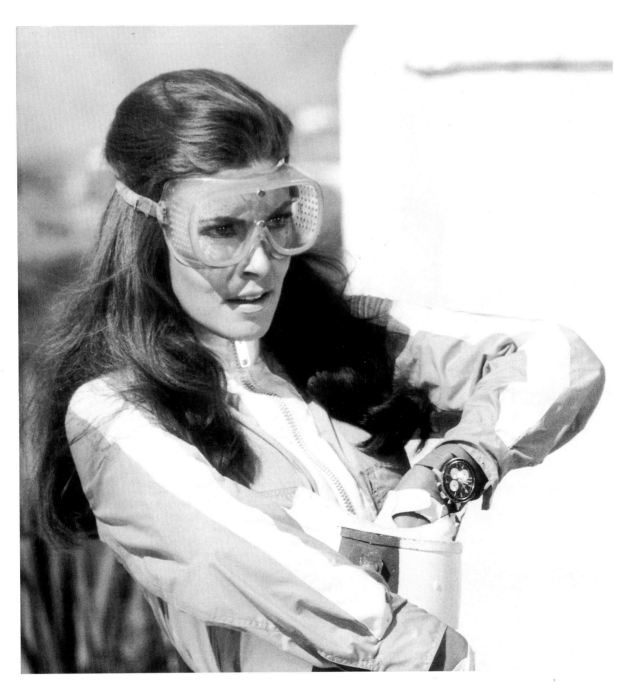

Raquel Welch with a Breitling Co-Pilot in the film "Fathom"

Opposite Page: Breitling advertisement, circa 1958, which appeared in the same firm in several languages. Bottom left: $400-500; Right, top to bottom: $1250, $1800, $2200.

Nur das Beste genügt im modernen Luftverkehr...

Sie alle wählen Breitling –
Schenken auch Sie Breitling Ihr Vertrauen!

Langjährige Erfahrung auf dem Gebiet der komplizierten Zeitmesser ermöglichte Breitling in Genf die Konstruktion dreier neuer
Uhren — Unitime, Navitimer und Chronomat — der führenden Chronographen unserer Tage. Der Fortschritt findet seinen Niederschlag
aber auch in der Breitling Automatic mit Kalender, der Uhr für den
anspruchsvollen Herrn, der im Alltag dieselbe Präzision verlangt wie
der Pilot für seine schwere Aufgabe.
Mit freundlichen Grüssen

**Ref. 66/26
Automatisch
mit Kalender
21 Steine
Ab Fr. 168.—**

Unitime, automatisch, zeigt
gleichzeitig die Stunde in allen Ländern
der Welt an. Eine aussergewöhnliche
Uhr für den modernen Geschäftsmann
(transatlantische Telefongespräche,
Luftreisen usw.). **Ab Fr. 272.—**

Navitimer, ein hochklassiger
Chronograph mit einem raffiniert aus-
gedachten Navigationsinstrument, gestattet die augenblickliche Berechnung
der Reisegeschwindigkeit, die Bestim-
mung der zurückgelegten Strecke usw.
und die Umwandlungen von Meilen in
Kilometer oder Seemeilen. **Fr. 277.—**

Chronomat, mit einer Rechenscheibe versehen, ist ein vollwertiges
Hilfsmittel für alle wichtigen mathematischen Operationen, wie Multiplikation, Division, Dreisatz, Zinsberechnung
usw. Er gestattet Ihnen die rasche Be-
stimmung der Durchschnittsgeschwin-
digkeit oder mittleren Rundenzeit.
Ab Fr. 237.—

BREITLING

GENÈVE

Breitling advertise-
ments, circa 1948. $500-
600 ea. Top watch,
$1200-1400. Bottom
watch, $1200-1400.

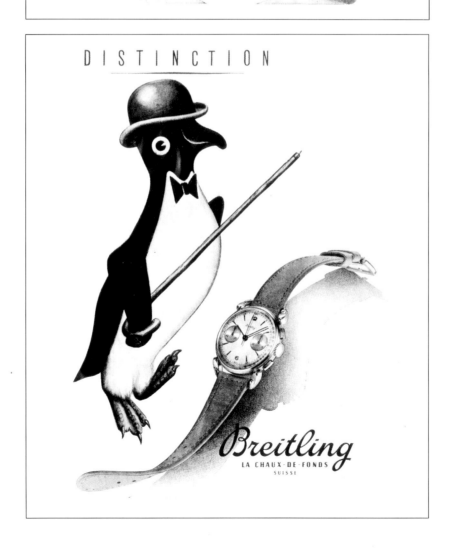

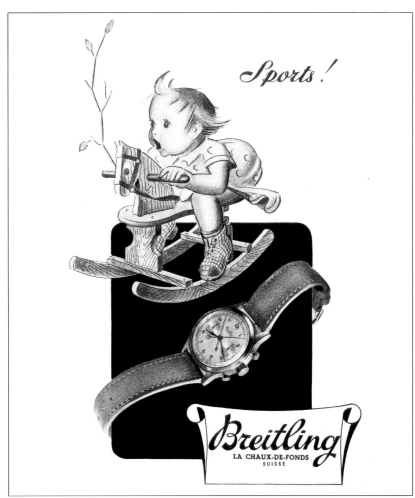

Breitling advertise-
ments, circa 1948.
Top: $800-1000; Bot-
tom: $850-950. top
watch, $1500-1600.
bottom watch,
$1500-1800.

A page from the 1946 catalog. Top row: $2000-2200,
$2000-2500; Bottom row:
$3000-3500, $2800-3000.

At the beginning of the sixties, the firm devoted a new series of watches, called "Top Time",
to young people. Breitling had correctly recognized that the future belongs to the young, and a
market analysis showed that more than 50% of
buyers were under 25 years of age. The Breitling
firm picked up on this message and accepted the
challenge: young people wanted watches that
matched their styles, and the Top Time series
filled the bill. Chronographs with the usual engineering but designed for the young came onto
the market. These modern, stylish designs com-
bined with time-tested Breitling precision were a
success.

Breitling "Super Ocean" diver's watch (left). $400-450

Automatic diver's watch for men (right). $450-500

Automatic diver's watch for ladies (left). $300-350

Breitling "Datora" (right). $800-1000

Breitling "Top Time". Bottom left: $700-800, bottom right: $900-1000.

"Top Time" series. Left to right: $700-850, $1500-2000, $700-850, $700-850

"Sprint" series. Left to right: $1500-1800, $700-850, $800-900, $700-850

"Top Time" series. Left to right: $700-850, $700-850, $800-850, $800-850

"Top Time" series. $700-850 ea.

Man's watch, circa 1952 (left). $200-250

"Chronomat", first version, 1942 (right). $2000-2200

Breitling-Wakmann Chronograph (left). $1200-1500

Man's wristwatch, circa 1948 (right). $200-250

Breitling chronograph, circa 1942 (upper left). $500-600

Breitling chronograph, circa 1942 (upper right). $500-600

Chronomat, 1944 version (right center). $1500-1800

Breitling chronograph, circa 1948 (lower right). $700-850

Breitling chronograph, circa 1942 (left). $1400-1600

Breitling chronograph, circa 1954 (upper left). $750-850

Breitling Chronograph, circa 1940 (upper right). $1200-1500

Breitling chronograph, circa 1944 (left center). $750-850

Breitling "Datora" with full calendar, circa 1952 (bottom left). $2000-2500

Breitling "Premier" chronograph, circa 1948. $800-1000

45

Breitling "Super Ocean" diver's watch with screwed-on crown, waterproof to 200 meters, circa 1972. $450-500

Breitling "Pult" chronograph with the crown by the 12, circa 1974. $400-450

"Chrono-Matic" automatic, circa 1970 (below). $800-900

"Chrono-Matic" automatic, circa 1975 (below). $700-800

"Chrono-Matic" with markings for sailing, circa 1969. $800-850

"Navitimer", hand-wound, with date (Valjoux 7740), circa 1976 (below). $900-1000

"Navitimer", LED version, indication automatically turns itself off after three seconds, as the batteries would otherwise be drained, circa 1976. $200-300

"Cosmonaute" automatic in large case, circa 1972. $2200-2500

Chronomat automatic with white dial, Breitling Caliber 11, circa 1970 (upper left). $1100-1200

Breitling "Super Ocean" diver's watch, circa 1971 (upper right). $800-900

Chronomat automatic in large case with white dial, circa 1972 (right center). $1500-1800

"Chrono-Matic" with pulse-rate scale, automatic Breitling Caliber 12, circa 1974 (lower right). $1200-1500

"Cosmonaute", hand-wound, in large case, circa 1968 (lower left). $1500-1800

In 1969, after four years of joint development, Breitling introduced an "automatic chronograph", a mechanical chronograph with automatic winding. The cooperating firms had succeeded in producing a watch that united a chronograph mechanism and a movement with automatic winding in one movement. The result of this development was a watch that became known under the name of "Chronomat." This movement had the general caliber designation of 11. It was also marketed by Breitling as Caliber 11. The impressive sum of some 500,000 Swiss francs was invested in this project by the firms of Breitling, Heuer-Leonidas and Hamilton-Büren, as well as by Dubois et Depraz. Production was carried on simultaneously by two firms. The basic movement was produced by the Büren firm in Büren, and the chronograph section by the firm of Dubois et Depraz in Le Lieu, so the firms of Breitling, Heuer, and Hamilton had nothing to do with making the raw movements. These movements were then delivered to these firms needing only finishing and installation into their cases. Willy Breitling and the other men in charge also met at regular intervals in Neuenburg during the developmental phase in order to make decisions and deal with any problems that had occurred during the course of development. The decisions regarding the design of the basic movement was that of Büren's technical director at that time, H. Kocher. The development of this watch movement was a sensation for the Swiss watch industry.

Moreover, it was demonstrated that developing and producing a product in cooperation can work without any of the involved firms having to give up its independence. From now on, Breitling offered a new chronograph series, the "Chronomat-Chrono-Matic", in its program. Some 300,000 were produced in all. The movement, with the caliber number 11 and the speed of 19,800 BPH, was then reworked again by Breitling, and the Caliber 12, with 21,000 BPH, appeared on the market. The technical features will be discussed in depth later. Here, as so many times before, Breitling was once again blazing the trail for a new generation of watches. Willy Breitling could justly be proud of his firm and what it had achieved.

In the years that followed, there was at first nothing new from Breitling. They continued to produce watches, and the age of electronics began. Watches that no longer ticked audibly appeared on the market in great numbers. One could no longer overlook these first signs of a new chapter in watch history. It was necessary to make changes and adapt to meet new demands. So, although at first with some hesitation and uncertainty, the production of quartz watches began at Breitling. In 1975 Breitling's offerings included, besides mechanical watches, a quartz version of the Chronomat in large and small cases with the same complications. Other watches followed.

A year later, a quartz version of the Navitimer came on the market, at first with then popular LED indication. Shortly thereafter, the same watch, but now with LCD indication, appeared. For sporting uses, Breitling introduced the Split and the Mini-Split. These stopwatches, needed for important sporting events, had the capability of timing up to 1/1000 of a second. As before, Breitling was still the official timepiece for major bicycle races such as the Tour de France, Tour d'Espagne, Tour d'Italia and others. Still it was not easy to adapt to this new technology, and the resulting difficulties became greater and greater.

In August, 1979 the entire Breitling firm was closed. One can read about it in the "L'Information Horlogère Suisse" journal of August 27, 1979: The end after almost 100 years. The eighteen employees in La Chaux-de-Fonds and six employees in Geneva had already received their termination notices toward the end of 1978. The low-priced offerings from the Far East, the price war, the inflated Swiss franc, the increasing shift to electronic watches by the public, and finally the illness of Willy Breitling, are the basic reasons that caused him to close down his firm. Voluntarily closing the firm prevented a public auction of the remaining property.

BREITLING GENÈVE

Das Ereignis, von dem wir Ihnen hier berichten, ist für unser Unternehmen und mich persönlich eine grosse Freude. Denn es ist in einem Klima gereift, das uns allen zeigt, wie sehr die Zeiten sich geändert haben ! Gemeinsam ist uns das Schwierigste gelungen – ich meine damit nicht etwa die Entwicklung einer Uhr, sondern unsere Teamarbeit !

Nun ist also bewiesen, dass drei Uhrenfabriken – ohne auf ihre Eigenständigkeit zu verzichten – gemeinsam vollbringen können, was keine von ihnen allein zu unternehmen vermag. Die Uhren-Archeologie interessiert niemanden. Begnügen wir uns mit der Feststellung, dass der Aufstieg unseres Unternehmens, das mein Grossvater vor rund hundert Jahren gründete, mit dem Start der ersten Flugzeuge zusammenfällt.

Vor dreissig Jahren schon haben wir dazu beigetragen, die Normen der Flugchronometrie zu definieren. Unser Flugzeug-Bordchronograph trägt in sich alle Vervollkommnungen die ihn vom Propellerflugzeug bis zu den Superjets geführt haben. Unsere Marke ist heute der offizielle Ausrüster für die Luftfahrtindustrie der ganzen Welt, und die Piloten schwören auf unseren Navitimer. Die technische Revolution und der Aufschwung des Sports haben uns gleichermassen angespornt, Instrumente für immer noch viel-

seitigere Aufgaben zu entwickeln. Wir haben den Chronomat geschaffen, der ein Chronograph ist, und den Chronoslide, der eine Stoppuhr ist. Beide sind mit einer Rechenscheibe ausgerüstet. Wir haben eine aussergewöhnlich komplette Reihe von Top Time-Chronographen produziert, wozu auch die erste Kollektion von quadratischen und Formuhren gehört. Damit haben wir die begeisterte Zustimmung der Jugend gewonnen, die einen phantastischen Markt darstellt, und gleichzeitig haben wir das Tor zur Mode aufgestossen : sogar die weibliche Kundschaft zeigt lebhaftes Interesse.

Schliesslich sind wir in der Elektronik heimisch geworden, indem wir drei Instrumente zur Messung kurzer Zeiten herausbrachten : den Electrosplit, einen quarzgesteuerten Zeitmesser mit Digitalanzeige, sein Zusatzgerät, den Printer, der die Zeiten auf einem Papierstreifen registriert, und schliesslich den Minisplit, einen wahren „Digest" des Electrosplit, – den kleinsten und leichtesten unter den elektronischen Zeitmessern mit numerischer Anzeige. Wenn wir nun gemeinsam mit unseren Freunden von Hamilton-Büren und Heuer-Leonidas den ersten automatischen Chronographen auf den Markt bringen, ist dies die Krönung unseres Werkes.

Auf dieser Erde gibt es nichts, das jemals abgeschlossen wäre. Bestimmte Abschnitte in der Entwicklung einer Marke aber entscheiden über ihre Zukunft. Wir erleben heute ein Ereignis von kapitaler Bedeutung und Sie haben sicher Verständnis dafür, dass es uns in freudige Erregung versetzt.

Willy Breitling
General Direktor
G. Léon Breitling S.A.
Genève

Although all the property of the firm was sold, the sheer determination of Willy Breitling alone prevented the name from becoming history.

Willy Breitling probably foresaw this collapse and had planned how to keep this world-famous firm's name alive throughout the crisis; he must have felt that this 100 year old watchmaking firm could not end so simply. Was foresight based on an inner voice? Was it a simple faith in the name of Breitling? Or maybe it was faith in the rebirth of the mechanical watch. We do not know. Willy Breitling looked for a practical solution.

After attempts with other firms, one bid from Ernst Schneider of the Sicura firm was accepted. In April, 1979, a contract was signed, well before closing deadline. Ernst Schneider took over the names of Breitling and Navitimer and thus had the right to go on using Breitling as the firm's name. Combining the modern technology of the Sicura firm with Breitling's international renown was a practical solution to save the Breitling name. The sons of Willy Breitling, Gregory and Alain, were too young to participate in the survival of the firm, and later they became interested in other careers. Willy Breitling died in May of 1979, and so the first chapter of Breitling history came to an end.

The new, present day firm was officially registered as Breitling Montres S.A. on November 30, 1982, and was located in Grenchen. Ernest Schneider and Willy Breitling had negotiated a solution to assure the continuance of the Breitling name.

Introductory text by Willy Breitling for the introduction of the Chrono-Matic series in 1969.

Text for the press conference to introduce the
Chrono-Matic series in 1969

CHRONOMATIC
Conférence de presse
sous le patronage
de la Fédération Horlogère Suisse

DIE INITIANTEN DES GEMEINSCHAFTSWERKES

Drei Uhrenfirmen stellen heute - in Zusammenarbeit mit der Maschi-
nenfabrik Dubois et Depraz SA - das Ergebnis ihrer Gemeinschaftsar-
beit vor: den automatischen Chronographen. Seit 1965 entschlossen,
zusammenzuarbeiten, trugen die drei Partner gemeinsam die Gesamt-
heit der Kosten für die Entwicklung und Schaffung eines neuen Pro-
duktes. Sie bewiesen damit, dass es möglich ist, ohne Verzicht auf
die eigene Persönlichkeit gemeinsam eine Leistung zu vollbringen,
die jeder für sich allein nicht hätte verwirklichen können.

G. Léon Breitling S.A., Genf

Im Jahr 1884 vom Grossvater des heutigen Generaldirektors gegründet,
verzeichnete die Firma seit dem Auftauchen der ersten Flugzeuge eine
stete Entwicklung. Mit der Herstellung ihrer der ersten Bordchronometer
im Jahre 1937 und der in der Folge erzielten Vervollkommnung dieser
Geräte sowohl für Propellerflugzeuge als auch Düsenflugzeuge wurde
die Oehler Firma gewissermassen der Hoflieferant der Weltluftfahrt.

Gleichzeitig bewogen die stürmische Entwicklung der Technologie und
der sportlichen Wettkämpfe sowie die Steigerung der Kaufkraft, nament-
lich der Jugend, die Techniker von Breitling, neue Formen und Verwen-
dungsmöglichkeiten des Chronographen zu suchen. So entstanden die
Zeitmesser mit ringförmigem Rechenschieber, die Zeitmesser mit Digitalanzeige und die ersten Chronographen für die weibliche Kundschaft.
Heute beschäftigt die Firma 180 Angestellte und Arbeiter. Dank ihrer
Exporte wird der Ruf der Qualität und Präzision, den die schweizerische Uhrenindustrie zu Recht beansprucht, weit über unsere Grenzen
in alle Welt hinaus getragen.

Breitling Genève | Hamilton-Büren | Heuer-Léonidas   ./.

CHRONOMATIC
Conférence de presse
sous le patronage
de la Fédération Horlogère Suisse

PRAEZISION UND TECHNIK: SPITZENLEISTUNG DER SCHWEIZER
UHRENINDUSTRIE

Drei Uhrenfabriken verwirklichen eine völlig neuartige Uhr

Genf und New York, 3. März 1969 - Drei Schweizer Uhrenfirmen,
G. Léon Breitling SA, Hamilton-Büren Watch Company SA und
Heuer-Léonidas SA bringen heute eine Uhr auf den Markt, welche
die Vorteile des automatischen Aufzugs und des Chronographen, verbunden mit Datumanzeige, in einem Stück vereinigt. Diese Erfindung,
mit der sich die Schweizerische Uhrenindustrie an die Spitze des Fort-
schrittes auf dem Gebiete der Mikromechanik stellt, wird inskünftig
zwei grosse Verbraucherkategorien im gleichen Lager zusammenführen:
jene, die ihre Uhr nicht mehr von Hand aufziehen wollen, und jene,
die kurze Zeiten präzis messen möchten.

Zum besseren Verständnis dieser Neuheit sei kurz daran erinnert, dass
der automatische Aufzug einer normalen Uhr die Verwendung einer
Schwungmasse bedingt, die bei den Bewegungen des Armes oder Hand-
gelenkes die Feder spannt.

Damit aus einer Uhr ein Chronograph wird, muss das Sekundenrad vom
Werk unabhängig sein, damit es für die Zeitmessung ausgekuppelt und
das Ablesen der Zeit ausgekuppelt und wieder in die Nullstellung zu-
rückgebracht werden kann. Bei der traditionellen Bauweise liegen diese
beiden Mechanismen - Schwungmasse und Zähler - ausserhalb des Uhr-
werks, wodurch die Uhr hauptsächlich dicker wird. Die Verwendung

Breitling Genève | Hamilton-Büren | Heuer-Léonidas   ./.

2.

einer im Werk eingebauten Schwungmasse und eines ebenfalls im Werk
integrierten, miniaturisierten Zählers ermöglicht nunmehr die Synthese
der beiden Elemente.

Die Erfindung des automatischen Chronographen bietet erneut Gewähr
für das Ansehen der schweizerischen Uhrenindustrie. Wie Minister
Gérard F. Bauer, Präsident der Fédération horlogère suisse, anlässlich
der Weltpremiere dieser Neuheit betonte, legt sie im Zeitpunkt der
beschleunigten technischen und kommerziellen Entwicklung, im Zeitpunkt einer immer schärferen ausländischen Konkurrenz, Zeugnis von
der Entschlossenheit und Fähigkeit unserer Industriellen ab, konkurrenz-
fähig und wettbewerbsfähig zu bleiben - und zwar im aktivsten, im
offensivsten und im aggressivsten Sinne dieser Begriffe. Ausserdem ist
der Beweis erbracht, dass drei Uhrenfirmen gemeinsam eine technische
Leistung vollbringen können, die sie allein nicht zu vollbringen vermöchten - und zwar vom Prototyp
bis zum Fertigprodukt.

* * *

21.1.69/Wyc/rm/1002-375

Like Leon Breitling, Ernest Schneider applied his initiative to his new firm. His prior training was in the fields of electronics and microelectronics, and he recognized the trends in the industry towards his area of expertise and focused on electronic watches and quartz technology. He did not lose sight of the biggest problem of electronic watches: that of energy source. Creating a watch without a battery as its power source was his long-term goal. Also, much of his attention was devoted to the mechanical watch, which by now was strongly linked to the Breitling name. These were considerations for the future, which at that time were somewhat uncertain for this newly reorganized watch manufacturer. Now was the time to find the right path towards these goals.

What is the first priority when one takes over the leadership of a completely reorganized firm with a renowned name? First of all, one should win back the confidence of the established customers, who waited to see what would happen. It was also important to show that the firm's original philosophy had not changed under this new leadership. Breitling's special markets, such as air travel, horseback riding, underwater activity and sailing, were reaffirmed to the public. Of special focus were the flying sports, which had always held a high position in Breitling's commitment. As the prime supplier of many airline companies and suppliers, Breitling could also make use of their good past reputation. For an effective presence in the market, though, an assortment of high-performance products had to be established.

Conferences with the raw-movement suppliers were necessary, in order to obtain material. Specialist personnel were obtained, modern machinery and equipment had to be procured, and an effective distribution network had to be established. The old distributors in the various countries (such as the Trautmann firm in Germany) assured a smooth transition to the new situation. All of this took place quickly, and Breitling was on a successful course again.

It was also necessary to get to know the customers' needs and to leave nothing to chance in filling them.

First of all, pilots were conferred with, and this was a group of professionals with whom the firm had much in common. Ernest Schneider, a pilot himself, as was his son, understood the requirements of reliability and safety being necessary for survival in aviation. In the production of precision instruments, such as Breitling watches, this goes without saying.

In 1980 Breitling put the Jupiter, Pluton and Mars chronographs on the market, designed especially for pilots. Using quartz technology, these watches offered two time zones, analog and digital indications, 12- or 24-hour indication, a stopwatch with 1/100 second capability, date, alarm and a turning bezel with a calculator on which various particular calculations necessary in aviation could be made.

At the beginning of the eighties, the market called for electronic timepieces and, as a result, production at Breitling was concentrated heavily on the manufacturing of such watches. Yet the first indications of a new evaluation of mechanical watches could scarcely be overlooked just a few years later. Breitling followed these new tendencies very quickly, and the Chronomat, which had first been offered in 1942, was marketed again as a mechanical chronograph--with a somewhat changed appearance. What was missing from the package, though, was the complicated manual that previously had been indispensable if one wanted to make full use of the watch. The point in time for its reappearance was exactly right, for in 1984 the 100th anniversary of the Breitling firm's founding was celebrated. A short time later, in 1986, it was followed by a new version of the legendary Navitimer of the fifties, a mechanical chronograph with hand-winding. As of 1988, it was again available as a mechanical chronograph with automatic winding.

Since the new beginning, the program had grown considerably, and the days of individual information sheets with technical data on the manufactured watches were over. A complete catalog was printed in 1986, and on fifteen pages were more than fifty different models. A large number of the available chronographs were equipped with mechanical movements again.

At this time Breitling made a clear statement applying to sailing sports. Here, under the influence of Eric Tabarly, twice winner of the transatlantic races for solo sailing, a series of watches came into being that met the needs of sailors, and that bore his name. Something similar took place when a link with the Italian sporting-goods firm of Ellesse was made: The technology and know-how of Breitling and the designs of Ellesse became the basis of a completely new series of watches that blended sportiness with flexibility and precision.

Ernest Schneider took the old principles by which firms had formerly been led and cast them aside. With up-to-date marketing on an international scale, a re-structuring of leadership would be put off by Breitling's new owners.

The firm's success proved his strategy right. Breitling watches, with their typical, unmistakable appearance, are still sought and treasured all over the world as "instruments for professionals."

In 1988 Breitling introduced the World, a quartz watch with four movements working independently of each other. On three dials the watch indicated 24 hours, and on the fourth, twelve hours and, naturally, the date. This watch was intended for frequent travelers who did not want to reset their watches constantly. Shortly thereafter came the Emergency. This watch was equipped with an emergency transmitter which was capable of sending out a signal so rescue operations could be guided more quickly, whether in the polar regions, in the desert, or on the high seas. A series of other new creations followed, including a limited issue (279 pieces) of the Montbrillant, a chronograph with the old Venus 175 movement from the forties.

In 1990, development reached its peak with the Astromat model. The Astromat is a mechanical chronograph with automatic winding, 30-minute and 12-hour counters, month, weekday, date, leap-year and moon-phase indications.

And what will be next from Breitling? Let's wait and be surprised, for that is the best way to enjoy something completely new.

Thus Breitling has followed the path farther. Since the appearance of the first edition of this book in 1992, a series of new models have enriched the market.

The Old Navitimer QP with its perpetual calendar is an achievement of the highest quality. Here the firm had once again created a milestone in watch development with the Caliber 33, which is still the smallest mechanical chronograph movement in the world. This movement is also used in the Navitimer Airborne.

When Breitling applied for a patent on a sweep-hand mechanism in the early forties, the button that started the sweep hand was integrated into the crown. Today, half a century later, Breitling has once again brought out a sweep hand wristwatch; this one has an automatic movement with date and calculator, and the typical Navitimer appearance. It also offers 12-hour and 30-minute

Navitimer advertisement, circa 1974. $1500-1800

Ihr persönliches Armaturenbrett...

NAVITIMER — ein «intelligenter» Chronograph

(denn die Uhr ist passiv, der Chronograph hingegen aktiv)

Dieser WASSERDICHTE CHRONOGRAPH (5 atm.) MIT AUTOMATIC ist ein erstaunliches Instrument. Betrachten Sie sein Zifferblatt:
1.— Logarithmische Skalen eines Flugkomputers
2.— Kalender
3.— Totalisatoren bis 30 Minuten und 12 Stunden
Der NAVITIMER löst alle Probleme, die während eines Fluges, einer Auto-Rally oder einer Yacht-Regatta auftreten können (Dividieren, Multiplizieren, Berechnung einer Durchschnittszeit usw.)

NAVITIMER
Chrono-matic
Ref. 1806

Könnten Sie den hier abgebildeten NAVITIMER «entziffern»?
Er bietet die Lösung für eines der 16 Rechenprobleme, die in der mit jedem NAVITIMER gelieferten Gebrauchs-anweisung enthalten sind.
Problem: Stundengeschwindigkeit
    Bekannt: Zeitdauer = 35 Minuten
        Entfernung = 85 km.
    Unbekannt: die Geschwindigkeit
Die Ziffer 85 der weissen Skala wird der Ziffer 35 der schwarzen Skala gegenübergestellt.
Lösung: Gegenüber dem Stundenmerkzeichen MPH (das sich über der 12 Uhr-Ziffer befindet) können Sie 146 ablesen. Das ist die gesuchte Stundengeschwindigkeit!

Bitte senden Sie mir kostenlos Ihren neuen Farbkatalog
Name_____ Vorname_____
Adresse_____ Stadt_____

BREITLING
GENÈVE
Trautmann KG – Breitling-Service, 75 Karlsruhe, Ebertstrasse 49

elapsed time indication. The movement, like the Caliber 33, has a diameter of 25.60 mm, equal to 11.5 lignes, and a height of 6.90 mm. The wheels turn in 39 jewels, and the movement has a massive gold rotor. The chronograph, and the sweep hand as well, are controlled by a column wheel.

Breitling, today in its fifth generation, has devoted itself to aviation more than ever. Eighty years after the first loopings of Nesterov, Pegoud and Beachy, the "Breitling World Cup of Aerobatics" was introduced in 1993 with the first official world prize competition of the Fédération Aeronautique Internationale. Here the pilots fly a free-style program lasting four minutes, which is evaluated by judges from various countries. The FAI has recognized this Breitling World Cup as having the same status as a world championship. Here the highest level of precision flying is required.

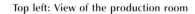

Top left: View of the production room

Center left: Final assembly; the rotor is just being installed

Bottom left: Emblem of the World Cup of Aerobatics, 1994

Top right: Waterproof testing

Bottom right: Breitling CAP 231 and Breitling CAP 231 EX

Bottom center: Ernest Schneider in the cockpit

Breitling, circa 1938. $1100-1200   Breitling watch, circa 1939. $1200-1400

Breitling Watches

Though watches were originally produced wholly by Breitling with the firm's own movements, they later quickly realized that it was not necessary for one firm to make everything themselves. Ultimately all that mattered was that the finished product attained the same high quality levels that would be there if Breitling had manufactured the product itself, but for a lower price. Producing raw movements had become very expensive and was still so. If one compares the number of raw-movement producers in the 1940s with the number today, only a few have remained. Breitling limited itself fairly early to buying the necessary parts and then assembling and completing the watches. Modifications, refinements, and finish were added to the raw movements at the Breitling factory, so that in the end the watch would deserve the Breitling name.

A number of firms made raw movements usually for several watch manufacturers at the same time. Breitling bought many raw movements manufactured from the firm Venus. They had a good reputation and guaranteed quality. Yet these raw movements could be installed into just any case or a case from Breitling. Other movements that Breitling bought came from FEF, FHF, Valjoux or ETA.

The watches produced by Breitling are divided into individual categories in this book, each of which is treated independently. It begins with stopwatches or pocket watches. These were at first worn on a chain or a band. Only later did watches appear that could be worn on the arm. The watches became smaller in terms of case measurements, and that also made them more attractive for the broad public. Since the wristwatch was at first slow to be accepted by men it was the ladies who, probably also influenced by fashion, first bought wristwatches in favor of watches that could be worn around the neck or on a chain.

Since the twenties when watches were first made to be worn on the arm, there were little improvisations in case shapes, winding mechanisms or band attachments. Early on, the wristwatch had become a definite genre with a defined shape, winding mechanism and band attachment.

Since the twenties, men's and women's watches for sports people, military people, aviators, rally drivers, etc., have been developed. With the simpler men's and women's wristwatches, it was fashion that dictated the ultimate design. In sports, it was the specific timing needs of the type of sport. The military was equally interested in having its own specialized types of watches with luminous hands, large winding crowns and protected cases, all with specific sizes for their needs. The same is true of watches used in aviation, motor sports and industry, for here too, specific types of dials and cases were required.

The fact that Breitling had a remarkably wide selection of watches for sale can be seen in the catalogs and advertisements used over the years. These are reproduced in the various sections of the material that follows.

Stopwatches

Stopwatches are made to measure small amounts of time or to add up several small amounts of elapsed time segments. In other words, they stop and record and measure small amounts of time. They have a mechanical movement, usually with one sweep seconds hand and then one or two small subsidiary hands. The longest hand is the one that indicates the smallest amount of time with the greatest possible accuracy. With the various types, time of 1/5, 1/10, 1/50 or 1/100 of a second can be measured as the smallest unit. The subsidiary hands are arranged so that the one can add up the elapsed minutes and the hours. The minute indication can go up to 15, 30, 45 or 60 minutes. The button arrangements can be with one to three buttons. These operate the simple stopwatch, the stopwatch with independent zero setting, the stopwatch with central minute addition, the stopwatch with double or sweep hand, and the split seconds chronograph. On the one-hand stopwatch with only one operating button, starting, stopping, and returning to zero are all done with the same button in order. No running record of elapsed time can be recorded. The next generation is equipped with a separate button for returning the hand to zero, and starting and stopping the chronograph are controlled by depressing the crown. With this the timing can be stopped or started freely, with the independent return button used to set the hands back to zero and total elapsed time can be totalled. Some stopwatches with sweep hands have another second hand under the first that is "dragged along" when started but can be stopped at any time, while the other second hand keeps moving and can be stopped at a different time, allowing for timing of two simultaneous events. Zero setting is generally done to both hands at the same time. The scales on the dials can be made to special requirements, being laid out for sporting, industrial or military uses. It was with these type of stop watches that Leon Breitling began his career, and so they properly have a premier standing at the commencement of over a hundred years of production.

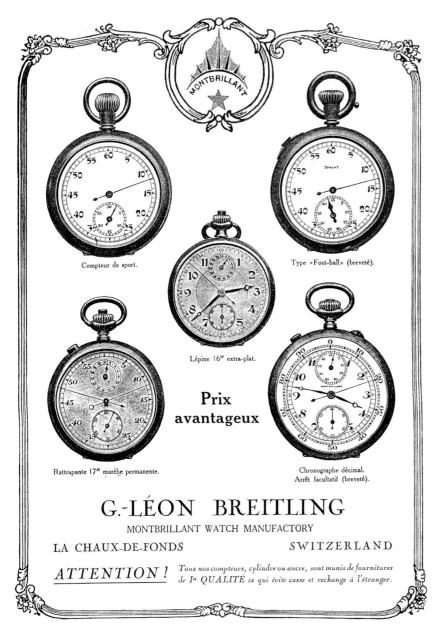

Compteur de sport.

Type «Foot-ball» (breveté).

Lépine 16''' extra-plat.

Prix avantageux

Rattrapante 17''' marche permanente.

Chronographe décimal.
Arrêt facultatif (breveté).

G.-LÉON BREITLING
MONTBRILLANT WATCH MANUFACTORY

LA CHAUX-DE-FONDS   SWITZERLAND

ATTENTION !   *Tous nos compteurs, cylindre ou ancre, sont munis de fournitures de I^a QUALITÉ ce qui évite casse et rechange à l'étranger.*

Breitling catalog, circa 1910, lent by Auktionen Joseph. Top row: $200-250 ea.; Center: $350-400; Bottom row: $300-350 ea.

COMPTEURS DE SPORTS
SPORTUHREN — TIMERS

N° 1.

Modèle enregistrant
30 minutes.
Ancre ou cylindre
Se fait en lépine Nickel,
Acier, Argent
cuvette glace ou métal.
Toutes formes
de boîtes.

N° 2.

Mouvement Cylindre 18'''
6 rubis
de notre Compteur
de Sport,
garanti simple, solide, facile
à réparer.
Fonctions absolument
sûres.

PRIX TRÈS AVANTAGEUX

COMPTEURS DE SPORTS
SPORTUHREN — TIMERS

N° 3.

Ce modèle de pendant
ovale,
spécialement adapté pour
mécanisme de Compteur,
n'augmente pas
le prix de la montre
et présente cet article sous
une forme très
élégante.

N° 4.

Mouvement ancre 18'''
7 rubis
antimagnétique.
Se fait aussi en qualité
supérieure, 11 rubis
garanti sous tous les
rapports,
terminage soigné
Balancier à vis.

SEHR VORTHEILHAFTE PREISE

CHRONOGRAPHE DOUBLE-FACE

N° 37. Côté des heures.   N° 38. Côté du chronographe.

Tous autres genres de cadran sur demande. Se fait aussi sans compteur de minutes.

CHRONOGRAPHE COMPTEUR — RATTRAPANTE SPLIT-SECOND

Mouvement
spécial

Qualité
extra

N° 39.

DOPPELTE SECOND ZEIGER.

SPÉCIMENS DE DÉCORS

N° 52.   N° 53.

Argent Niellé avec et sans incrustation or.

N° 54.   N° 55.

Frappes artistiques Vieil argent. — *Grande variété de sujets sportifs.*

Stopwatches shown in the 1928 catalog. Left side: top to bottom, $175-200, $150-175, $1000-1100, $300-350; Right side: top to bottom, $175-200, $150-175, $250-1700 ea, $800-2000 ea,

59

CHRONOGRAPHES

16"

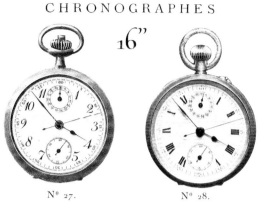

N° 27.   N° 28.

Mouvement 16''' ancre, sp. bt. 17 rubis.
Fonctions irréprochables. Métal, acier, argent, grande
variété de cadrans et boîtes.

Grandeur
naturelle

Poussoir de
Chronographe
indépendant

N° 29.

Mouvement soigné 16''' pour bracelet chronographe
sp. bt. 17 rubis bal. coupé, frein, aciers anglés, etc.

ASK FOR PRICES
DEMANDEZ NOS PRIX

— 22 —

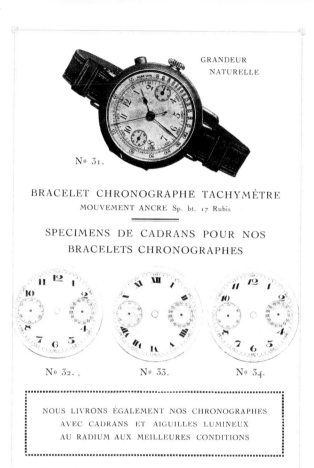

GRANDEUR
NATURELLE

N° 31.

BRACELET CHRONOGRAPHE TACHYMÈTRE
MOUVEMENT ANCRE Sp. bt. 17 Rubis

SPECIMENS DE CADRANS POUR NOS
BRACELETS CHRONOGRAPHES

N° 32.   N° 33.   N° 34.

NOUS LIVRONS ÉGALEMENT NOS CHRONOGRAPHES
AVEC CADRANS ET AIGUILLES LUMINEUX
AU RADIUM AUX MEILLEURES CONDITIONS

ASK FOR PRICES • PRIX AVANTAGEUX
VERLANGEN SIE OFFERTEN

— 24 —

MONTRE DE DAMES
SECONDE AU CENTRE

MOUVEMENT
CYLINDRE

FABRICATION
SPÉCIALE

N° 48.

N° 49.   N° 50.

N° 51.

Ces montres se recommandent spécialement aux
infirmiers, sœurs d'hôpitaux, etc.

DEMANDEZ ÉCHANTILLONS ET PRIX

60

— 31 —

Sixteen-ligne chronograph caliber, circa 1928 (upper
left). Top row: $350-400 ea.; Bottom: $900-1000.

Wrist chronograph with anchor movement, circa 1932
(upper right). $800-1000

Left: Ladies' watches with second hands, circa 1930.
Clockwise: $800-900, $250-300, $250-300, $250-300.

Opposite page:
Large chronograph catalog (from Breitling), circa 1930.
Top: top row, $350-400, $350-400, $350-400; Bottom
row: $375-400, $375-400. Bottom: top row, $350-450,
$350-450, $350-450, $350-450; bottom row: $350-
450, $350-450.

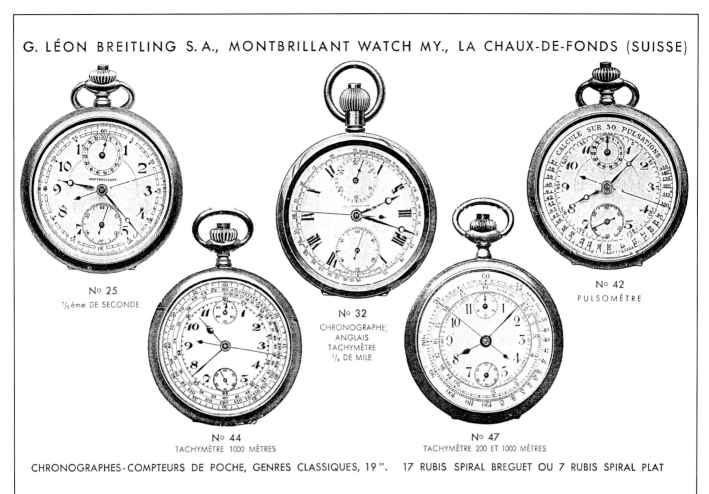

No 25
1/5ème DE SECONDE

No 32
CHRONOGRAPHE
ANGLAIS
TACHYMÈTRE
1/4 DE MILE

No 42
PULSOMÈTRE

No 44
TACHYMÈTRE 1000 MÈTRES

No 47
TACHYMÈTRE 200 ET 1000 MÈTRES

CHRONOGRAPHES-COMPTEURS DE POCHE, GENRES CLASSIQUES, 19'''.   17 RUBIS SPIRAL BREGUET OU 7 RUBIS SPIRAL PLAT

G. LÉON BREITLING S.A., MONTBRILLANT WATCH MY., LA CHAUX-DE-FONDS (SUISSE)

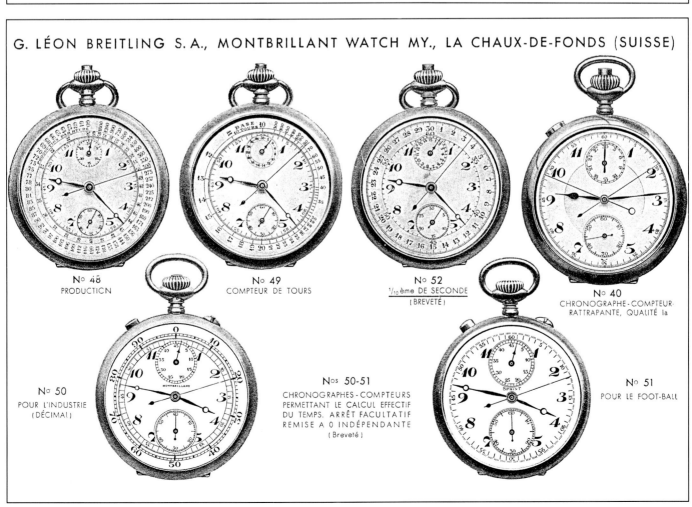

No 48
PRODUCTION

No 49
COMPTEUR DE TOURS

No 52
1/10ème DE SECONDE
(BREVETÉ)

No 40
CHRONOGRAPHE-COMPTEUR-
RATTRAPANTE, QUALITÉ Ia

No 50
POUR L'INDUSTRIE
(DÉCIMAL)

Nos 50-51
CHRONOGRAPHES-COMPTEURS
PERMETTANT LE CALCUL EFFECTIF
DU TEMPS. ARRÊT FACULTATIF
REMISE A 0 INDÉPENDANTE
(Breveté)

No 51
POUR LE FOOT-BALL

No 57
18″′ EXTRA-PLAT
FANTAISIE-BISEAU

No 34 16″′ S/CUV.
GENRE JAPON

No 56
18″′ EXTRA-PLAT
CLASSIQUE LENT. BASS.

CHRONOGRAPHES-COMPTEURS DE POCHE EXTRA-PLATS

CHRONOGRAPHES DE POCHE
POCKET CHRONOGRAPHS · TASCHENCHRONOGRAPHEN

CHRONOGRAPHES DE POCHE
POCKET CHRONOGRAPHS · TASCHENCHRONOGRAPHEN

Les Nos 604, 626, 627 sont des chronographes de poche
EXTRA PLATS
et très élégants

The numbers 604, 626, 627 are fancy and
EXTRA FLAT
pocket chronographs

Die Nummern 604, 626, 627 sind
EXTRA FLACHE
und sehr elegante Taschenchronographen

No 650 Chronographe-compteur 1 poussoir avec aiguille
dédoublante et rattrapante, totalisateur 30 minutes
Split second chronograph 1 pusher, 30min. recorder
Doppelzeigerchronograph 1 Drücker, 30-Min-Zähler

No 644 Même modèle que No 643 mais avec totalisateur
12 heures
Same as No. 643 but with 12 hours recorder
Gleich wie Nr. 643 aber mit 12-Stundenzähler

No 643 Chronographe-compteur 2 poussoirs avec aiguille
dédoublante et rattrapante, totalisateur 30 minutes
*Split second chronograph, 2 pushers, 30 minutes
recorder*
Doppelzeigerchronograph 2 Drücker, 30-Min-Zähler

No 649 Même modèle que No 644 mais avec calendrier
simple et phases de lune
*Same as No. 644 but with simple calendar and
moon-phase*
Gleich wie Nr. 644 aber mit einfachem Kalender
und Mondphasen

Opposite page: From the large 1930 chronograph catalog (above) $400-500. $350-400. $400-500.

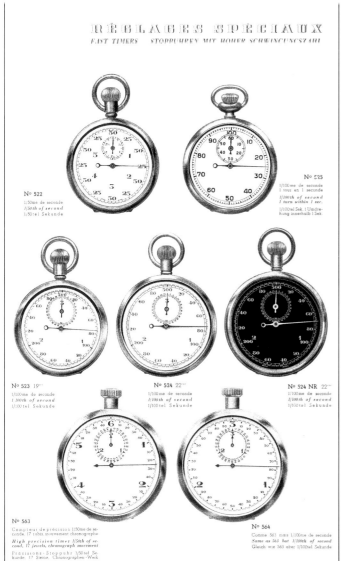

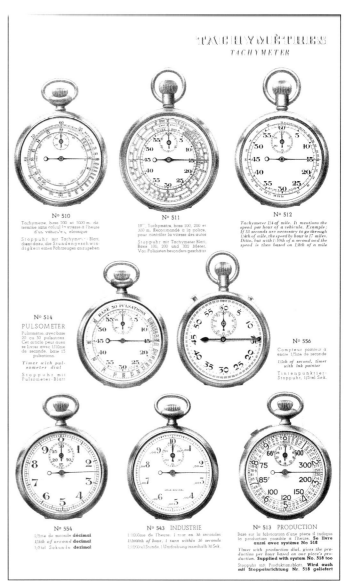

Stopwatches shown in the 1953 catalog. Left: Top row, $200-250 ea.; Center row, $200-250 ea.; Bottom row, $200-250 ea. Right: Top row, $250-300 ea.; Center row, $250-300 ea.; Bottom row, $250-300 ea.

Opposite page bottom: Pocket chronographs shown in the 1946 catalog. Top: left to right, $400-500, 400-500, Bottom left: $400-500 ea. Bottom right: top row, $800-1000 ea.; bottom row, $800-1000 ea.

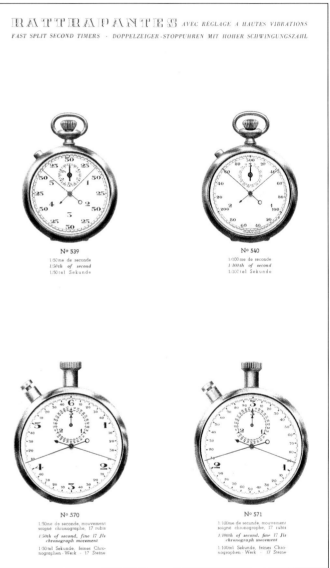

Double-hand stopwatches shown in the 1953 catalog.
Left: $250-300 ea. Right: $250-300 ea.

"Autotimer" stopwatch with tachometer scale, circa 1974 (left). $200-250

"Sprint" stopwatch with 1/5 second, in plastic case, circa 1972 (right). $200-250

"Chronoslide" stopwatch with turning lunette and calculator, circa 1969 (left). $225-250

"Sprint" stopwatch with 1/5 second, in metal case, circa 1972 (right). $200-250

"Yachting Timer" in metal case, circa 1972 (left). $400-500

"Tel-Rad" stopwatch for radio, television and film use, circa 1969. $225-250

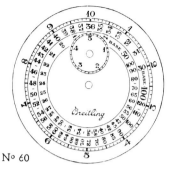

N° 60

Bases 50 et 100 m. et division décimale, 1/5e de sec.
50 and 100 m. bases and dec. division, 1/5th of sec.
Beobachtungsstrecken 50 od. 100 Meter u. Dezimal-
Einteilung und 1/5tel Sekunde.

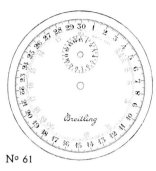

N° 61

Base 100 mètres et 1/10me de seconde
100 meters base and 1/10th of second
Beobachtungsstrecke 100 m u. 1/10tel Sek.

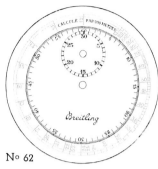

N° 62

Base 200 mètres et 1/5me de seconde
200 meters base and 1/5th of second
Beobachtungsstrecke 200 m u. 1/5tel Sek.

N° 63

Bases 200 et 1000 mètres et 1/5me de sec.
200 and 1000 meters bases and 1/5th of sec.
Beobachtungsstrecken 200 und 1000 Meter
und 1/5tel Sekunde

N° 64

Bases 100, 200 et 300 m. et 1/5me de sec.
100, 200 and 300 m. bases and 1/5th of sec.
Beobachtungsstrecken 100 - 200 u. 300 M.
und 1/5tel Sekunde

N° 65

Base 1000 m. sur 4 tours et 1/5me de sec.
1000 m. base on 4 min. and 1/5th of sec.
1000 Meter Beobachtungsstrecke innerhalb 4 Minuten und 1/5tel Sekunde

N° 66

Tachymètre et télémètre et 1/5me de sec.
Tachy- and telemeter and 1/5th of sec.
Tachy - Telemeter und 1/5tel Sekunde

N° 67

*English Tachymeter on 1/4th of
mile base and 1/5th of second*

N° 68

*English Tachymeter on 1/8th of
mile base and 1/10th of second*

N° 69

Tachymètre DCA 1/25me de seconde, 1 tour en 10 secondes
A.A. Defense Tachymeter 1/25th of second, 1 turn within 10 seconds
Flak-Tachymeter 1/25tel Sekunde, 1 Umdrehung innerhalb 10 Sek.

N° 70

Tachymètre mètres/secondes et 1/30me de sec., 1 tour en 10 sec.
Meter/sec. Tachymeter and 1/30th of sec., 1 turn within 10 sec.
Meter/Sek. Tachymeter u. 1/30tel Sek., 1 Umdr. innerhalb 10 Sek.

**Various dial patterns for
chronographs and stop-
watches with scales, still
used today**

Si ces cadrans spéciaux sont désirés, prière de se référer
aux numéros ci-dessus
When passing orders kindly state above reference numbers
Bei Bestellungen bitte Referenznummern angeben

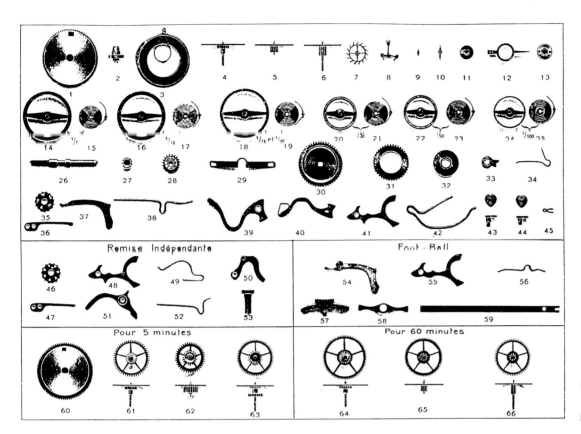

Spare parts for an 18-lignes stopwatch

Remise Indépendante

Foot-Ball

Pour 5 minutes

Pour 60 minutes

Ersatzteile für
STOPPUHR
Kaliber 18 lig.

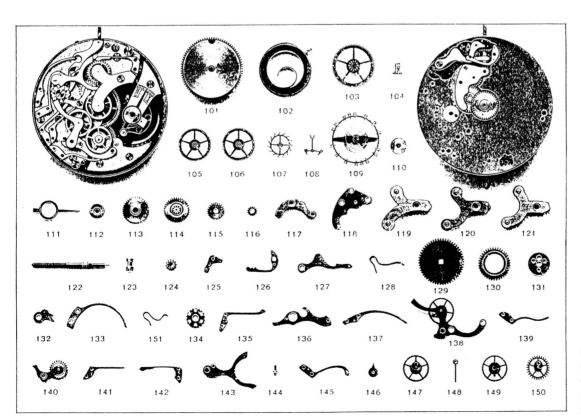

Spare parts for a 17-lignes chronograph

Ersatzteile für
CHRONO-
GRAPH
Kaliber
17 lig. EC

Various stopwatches from the big 1969 catalog. $100-150 ea.

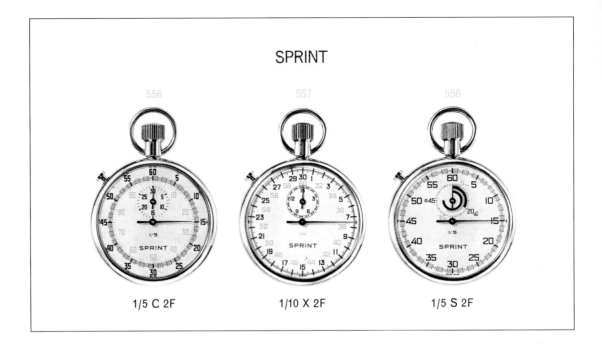

SPRINT

556   557   558

1/5 C 2F   1/10 X 2F   1/5 S 2F

Circa 1972, $75-100

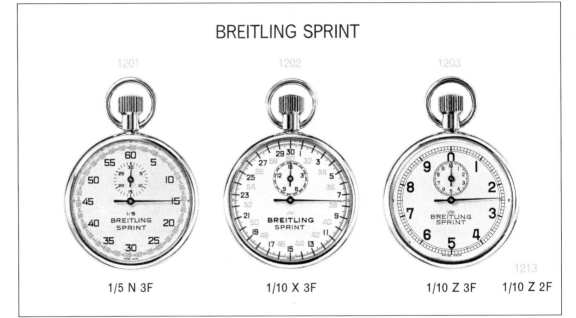

BREITLING SPRINT

1201   1202   1203

1213

1/5 N 3F   1/10 X 3F   1/10 Z 3F   1/10 Z 2F

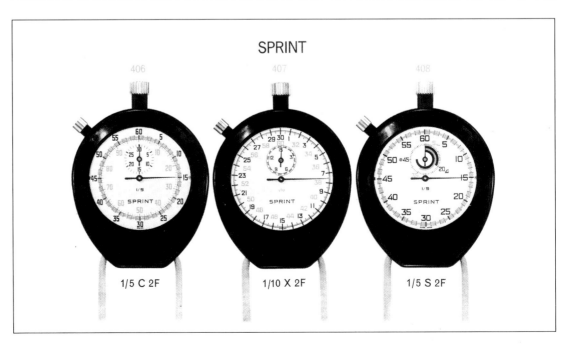

SPRINT

406   407   408

1/5 C 2F   1/10 X 2F   1/5 S 2F

Men's Wristwatches

Here we include all men's wristwatches that do not include some additional function such as subsidiary dials or start stop mechanisms, such as are commonly found in chronographs. They are simple but certainly beautiful watches, generally set in conservatively styled cases that suit the fashions of their times. The catalog of 1946 shows such watches; they are striking on account of their imaginative band attachments, which corresponded to the fashion of the time.

There were 32 different models offered, in gold, nickel or chrome-plated cases. Waterproof watches were also included in their line at that time. The bands are almost all made of leather, but a few steel ones can also be found.

Most of these watches were still included in the firm's program in the fifties and even later, though they were not as widely known as the Breitling chronographs. Specialties in these watches are found in numbers 94/28, 88/128 and 93/88, as well as 84/28, 85/28 and 86/28. These are watches with date, calendar and moon phase.

Another watch that has become somewhat famous is the Breitling "Unitime", with the catalog number 1/260. This watch features a gold or steel case, an automatic movement, a date and time indication for 24 cities around the world engraved in the turning bezel and, of course, the local time as well. The development of this interesting mechanism is attributed to Louis Cottier. The turning ring is driven only at half the speed of the hands, resulting in the 24-hour division. In the sixties and seventies, uncomplicated men's watches fell to a disinterested public. It is only under the new Breitling leadership that more of them have been on the market.

The various Breitling products of this period can be seen on the following pages.

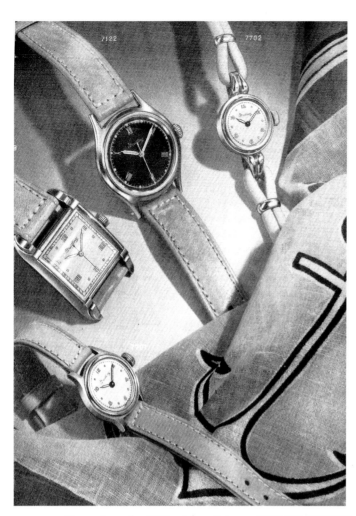

Above: From the 1946 catalog. Top row: $100-125, $250-300, $200-250, $100-125, $200-250, $150-200, $250-300. $200-250.

Below: From the 1952 catalog. Left row: top to bottom, $200-225 ea.; Center row: top to bottom, $200-225, $200-225; Right row: top to bottom, $200-225 ea.

Opposite page: From the big 1952 catalog of men's wristwatches. 1st row: left to right, $300-400, $300-400, $2000-2200, $1900-2100; 2nd row: $2000-2200, $200-225, $200-225; 3rd row: $200-225, $200-225, $200-225, $100-125, $100-125; 4th row: $100-125, $100-125; 5th row: $400-450, $400-500, $200-225, $200-225, $200-225; 6th row: $350-500, $200-225, $100-125, $100-125.

BREITLING

GENÈVE

Opposite page: The 1952 Breitling catalog of ladies' and men's wristwatches. 1st row: left to right, $225-250 ea.; 2nd row: $225-250 ea.; 3rd row: $200-250, $225-250, $225-250, $225-250; 4th row: $200-250, $225-250, $225-250, $225-250; 5th row: $350-450, $1500-1800.

Men's wristwatches from the 1946 catalog. $225-250 ea.

2906/29

2900/29

2905/29

2506/25

2501/25

BREITLING
GENÈVE

1060/29

2505/25

2504/25

2507/25

1059/29

2503/25

238/25

236/25

769

Waterproof automatic watches with gold case and calendar, circa 1954. Left: $400-500; Top right: top row, $200-225 ea., bottom row, $500-600; Bottom right: $400-500 ea.

2521
18 ct. gold

2601   2602   2603

CALENDAR WATERPROOF AUTOMATIC

ROOF AUTOMATIC

2604

2606   18 ct. gold

2605
18 ct. gold

B

BREITLING
GENÈVE

Man's wristwatch, circa 1952 (left). $200-225

Man's wristwatch, circa 1960 (right). $200-225

Man's wristwatch, circa 1954 (left). $200-225

Man's wristwatch, circa 1958 (center). $300-400

Man's wristwatch, circa 1949 (right). $200-225

Man's wristwatch, circa 1970 (left). $200-225

Man's wristwatch, circa 1954 (right). $200-225

75

Man's wristwatch, circa 1960 (above). $125-150

Man's wristwatch, "Navitimer" with date, circa 1958 (right center). $200-225

Man's wristwatch "Unidate" in square case with date, circa 1966. $250-300

Man's wristwatch, circa 1969 (left). $200-225

Man's wristwatch, circa 1948 (right). $200-225

Valjoux Caliber 23 movement. $1000-1100   **Venus Caliber 175 movement. $1000-1100**

Opposite page: "Unitime" (upper left) with 12- and 24-hour indication, circa 1952

Various men's wristwatches, all circa 1952. Top row: left to right, $500-600, $200-225, $200-225; Center row: $200-225, $200-225, $200-225, $1200-1500; Bottom row: $200-225, $200-225, $1200-1500.

From the 1946 catalog. Clockwise: $250-300, $300-350, $225-250, $250-300.

UNITIME

Weltzeit Kalender-Automatic

Die Breitling-UNITIME wurde speziell für alle geschaffen, die viel und weit reisen: Geschäftsleute und Übersee-Touristen, vor allem aber Flug- und Schiffskapitäne! Es gibt keine andere Uhr, die — wie die UNITIME — in allen Einzelheiten so eindeutig auf ihren Bestimmungszweck ausgerichtet ist: sie ist automatisch, besitzt einen Kalender und eine mit dem Werke synchronisierte 24 Stunden-Skala und wird durch ein rostfreies, absolut wasserdichtes Stahlgehäuse geschützt! Zeiger und Zifferblatt sind nachtleuchtend. 21 Rubine, stoßsicher. Die auf dem drehbaren Glasring gravierten Zahlen, mit der 24-Stunden-Skala verglichen, dienen dazu, die Zeit in irgendeiner anderen Zeitzone bzw. an irgendeinem Ort der Welt unverzüglich abzulesen.

UNITIME Mod. 2610 Edelstahl DM 350.- *
Jeder UNITIME liegt eine ausführliche Gebrauchsanweisung bei.

❷

❻

❼❽

BREITLING
GENÈVE

BREITLING-Service für Deutschland 75 Karlsruhe · Postfach 1767

Die Traumuhr — transOcean

Auf dem einzigartigen Vertrauensverhältnis mit der Weltluftfahrt ist eine weitere Schöpfung Breitlings – die automatische TransOcean – aufgebaut. Das Herz der TransOcean ist ein vollautomatisches, stoßsicheres und antimagnetisches 25-Rubine-Werk von erstaunlicher Gangtreue.

Der große und kräftige Rotor der Automatvorrichtung ist in einem besonders widerstandsfähigen Lager eingesetzt. Er ist mit einem schweren Metallkranz versehen, was einen sicheren Aufzug gewährleistet.

Die TransOcean ist dank dem Durchmesser der Unruhe Glucydur außergewöhnlich präzis reguliert. Das Ganze umgibt ein höchst dichtes Gehäuse, in dessen Boden ein Echtheitszeichen eingraviert ist, welches Breitlings Zugehörigkeit zur Welt der Flieger bezeugt. In einem Wort: ein wertvoller, selten schöner Zeitmesser!

Herrenautomatic

mit Kalender, Selbstaufzug, 25 Rubine, wasserdicht, echte Goldziffern, in Luxusschatulle.

Mod. TO-1   Edelstahl mit schmiegsamem verstellbarem Edelstahlband . . . . DM 405.– *

Mod. TO-2   dto. mit massiver Goldkappe und Goldplaquéband . . . . DM 555.– *

. . . das Gegenstück für die Dame

Die Ganggenauigkeit einer Uhr ist ein Aspekt, der die Frau genauso interessiert wie den Mann. Die TransOcean für Damen ist das Gegenstück der TransOcean, wie sie für Herren geschaffen wurde. Als bahnbrechendes Modell ist die TransOcean für Damen der begeisterndste Ausdruck der Präzision BREITLING.

Selbstaufzug, 25 Rubine, wasserdicht, echte Goldziffern, in Luxusschatulle.

Mod. TO-5   Edelstahlgehäuse mit schmiegsamem, verstellbarem Edelstahl-Armband DM 350.– *

Mod. TO-6   Goldcap-Gehäuse mit schmiegsamem, verstellbar. Goldplaqué-Armband DM 470.– *

Mod. TO-7   18 Kt. Gold, echtes Crocoband DM 599.– *

Gold »CHRONOMETER«

die vollkommenste Schöpfung aus unserer Kollektion. Die automatische TransOcean in Chronometerausführung, amtlich geprüft, mit offiziellem Gangschein, schwerem wasserdichtem 18karätigem Goldgehäuse, Ziffern aus Gold, auf wunderschönem, mattversilbertem Zifferblatt. In Croco-Luxus-Geschenkschatulle.

Mod. TO-3   ohne Datum   Crocoband   DM 980.– *

Mod. TO-4   mit Datum   Crocoband   DM 999.– *

Opposite page: Advertisement for the "Trans-Ocean" as a dream watch; only a few of them were sold with chronometer certificates, although most of the watches attained the standards. Top right: $2500-2800; Bottom row: $2000-2400. $1500-1800. $1000-1200.

Breitling advertisement from 1954. Top row: $225-250, $150-175, $150-175, $400-500; Bottom row: $225-250, $225-250; Left row: $600-700, $600-800, $300-400; Right row: $225-250, $225-250.

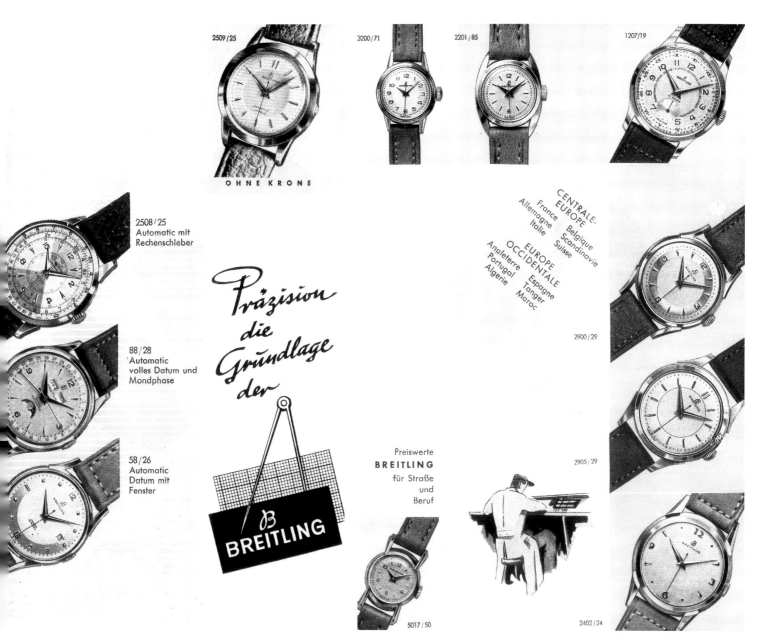

2509/25

OHNE KRONE

3200/71

2201/85

1207/19

2508/25
Automatic mit
Rechenschieber

88/28
Automatic
volles Datum und
Mondphase

58/26
Automatic
Datum mit
Fenster

*Präzision
die
Grundlage
der*

CENTRALE-
EUROPE
France   Belgique
Allemagne   Scandinavie
Italie   Suisse

EUROPE
OCCIDENTALE
Angleterre   Espagne
Portugal   Tanger
Algerie   Maroc

2900/29

2905/29

Preiswerte
BREITLING
für Straße
und
Beruf

BREITLING

5017/50

2402/24

Breitling advertisement from 1954. Left: top row, $225-250, $225-275 ; bottom row: $225-250, $225-250. Right: top right, $2200-2500, Center: $2000-2200, $2000-2200, $2500-2800, $2000-2200; Bottom left: $1500-1800.

MÄNNER SCHÄTZEN LEISTUNG—
Automatic · massiv Gold

2505/25

925/91

2501/25
Gold auf Stahl

MÄNNER WÄHLEN „BREITLING"

769

Stop - Uhr und
Rechenschieber

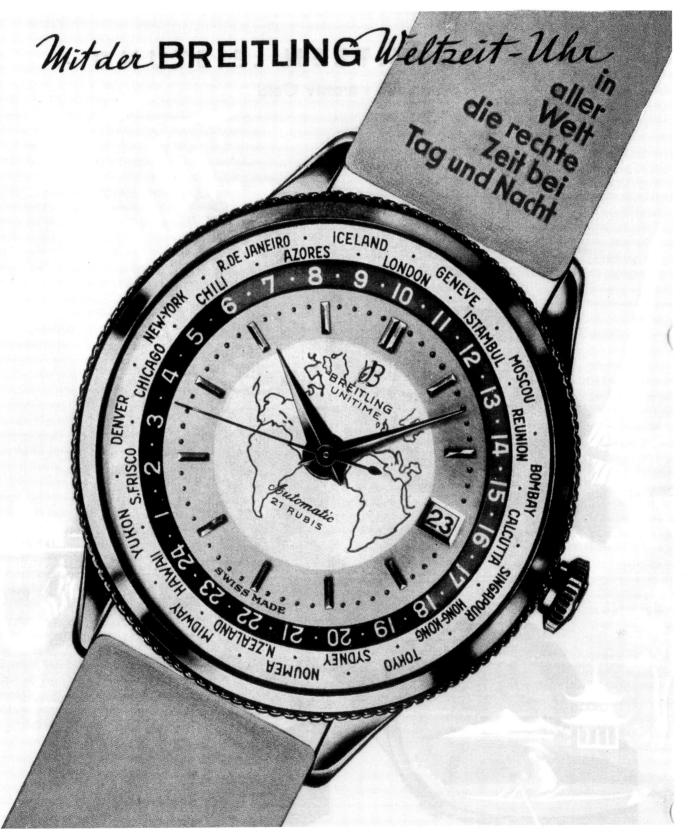

"Unitime", which also became known by the name "Worldtime". Its bezel, engraved with the names of cities, turns at half the normal speed; circa 1951. $2800-3000

Ladies' Wristwatches

Opposite page: Breitling advertisement for ladies' watches, circa 1952. Top row: $125-150 ea.; Center: $125-150 ea.; Center right: $125-150 ea.; Bottom left: $125-150, $200-250, $200-250, $200-250, $200-300, $200-300, $200-300.

To a greater extent than in other areas, the majority of ladies' watches can be regarded mostly as pieces of jewelry. With just a few small exceptions, ladies' watches with chronograph functions or waterproof models for water sporting uses are almost never to be found. The assortment of ladies' watches offered by Breitling has always been very small, but what was produced was well worth looking at: square and round case designs in gold, steel, or chrome-plated. Both hand-wound or automatic models were available. The case designs of ladies' watches have always been strongly influenced by fashion. The models of the forties up to the more recent years were very suited to the trends of the times and are sought-after collectors' items today. In their 1946 catalog, Breitling offered 23 variations, and in a catalog from the fifties there are almost fifty models. Except for a few "exotic" case designs, there were no unusual types of movements in that area. After 1979 Breitling continued to produce ladies' watches in the "Tarbarly Lady" and "Ellesse Lady" series, as well as the "J-Class Lady" and "Callistino" series in the 1991 catalog.

From the large 1952 catalog of ladies' watches. Left: top row, $200-300, $150-200, $200-300, $150-200, $200-250; bottom row, $250-300, $250-300, $150-200, $200-250. Right: $150-200.

Exclusive Modelle

IN MASSIV GOLD

NEUE MODELLE, NACH DENEN MAN SIE FRAGT...

BREITLING

GENF

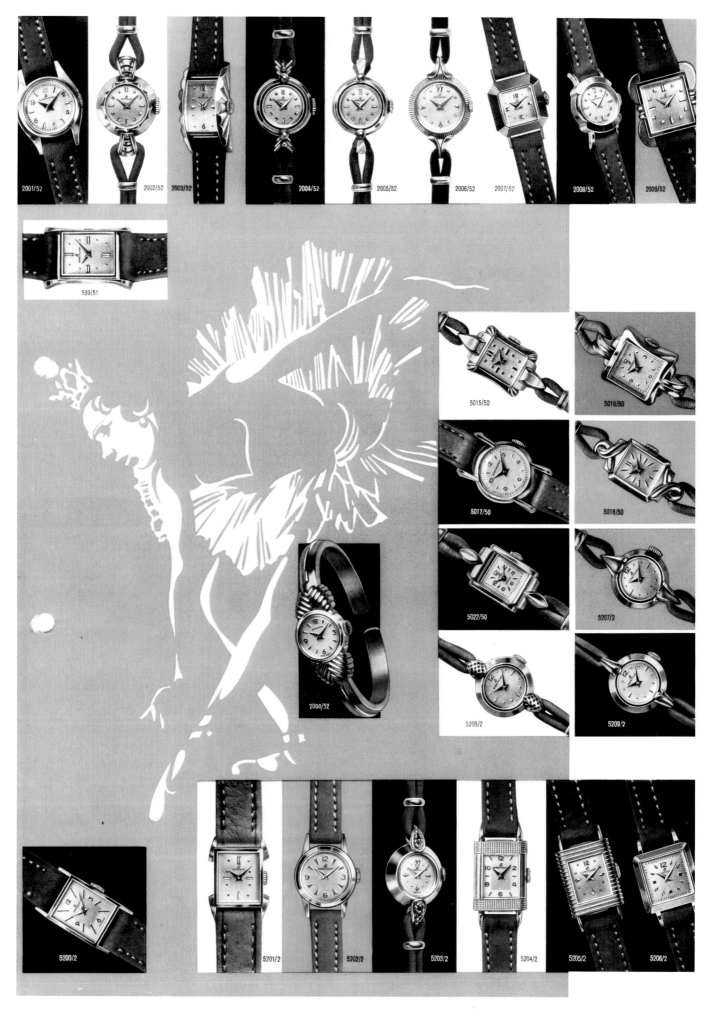

2001/52   2002/52   2003/52   2004/52   2005/52   2006/52   2007/52   2008/52   2009/52

599/51

5015/50   5016/50

5017/50   5018/50

5022/50   5207/2

2000/52

5208/2   5209/2

5200/2   5201/2   5202/2   5203/2   5204/2   5205/2   5206/2

ANJOU. Splendide création, torsade or et brillants, bracelet daim

ILE-DE-FRANCE Haute distinction classique, 4 brillants sur platine

SENSATION. Or 18 carats, heures or, dessin extrêmement harmonieux

CLAIRVAL Fine et précieuse avec bracelet daim noir

BLOIS. Création très originale et bracelet daim

VIRGINIE Or 18 carats, heures or, ligne de grandepureté

« *L'heure éblouissante* »

VÉNUS. Petit chef-d'œuvre rayonnantcom-

Several advertisements for ladies' watches, from the 1952-1956 period. 1st row: $175-200 ea.; 2nd row: $175-200 ea.; 3rd row: $350-400, $350-400, $350-400, $150-200, $150-200. 4th row: $175-200 ea.

5538

5537

5536

5545

5547

5549

5550

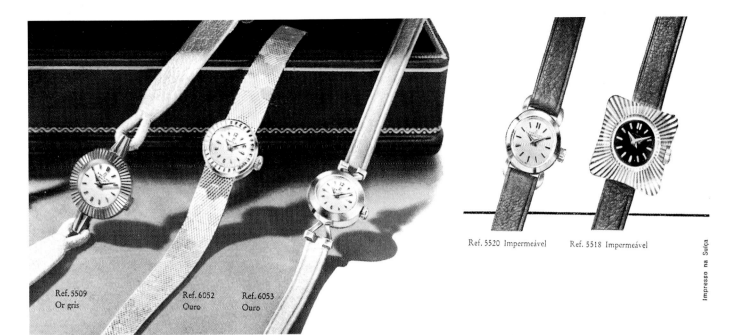

Impresso na Suíça

Ref. 5509
Or gris

Ref. 6052
Ouro

Ref. 6053
Ouro

Ref. 5520 Impermeável   Ref. 5518 Impermeável

Ladies' watches of 1956 (above). $150-225. $150-225. $150-225. $175-225. $150-250.

Ladies' watches of 1936. Clockwise: $175-225 ea.

No other Watch Company in the World can make this Claim

The Breitling Watch Company, through its research and development for the U. S. Government and various military services, has become THE WORLD'S LEADING MANUFACTURER of precision timepieces in the aviation industry. Besides having supplied accurate timepieces to the U. S. Government, we are presently supplying all major airframe manufacturers, airlines and A. O. P. A., with various types of precision timing devices and instruments, including those illustrated on these pages.

BREITLING

Qualified Supplier to the U.S. Military and to the majority of the World's Aircraft Manufacturers and Airlines

NAVITIMER — 17 Jewel, exclusive chronograph, calibrated with logarithmic scales of an aerial navigation computer. Movable bezel; 12 hour recorder; 30 minute register; luminous dial.
8060 Stainless steel.

8061 Gold filled.

8062 18 Kt. gold.

COPILOT — 17 Jewel, all steel waterproof chronograph. Unique 15 minute register for close timing, and 12 hour recorder. Large, easy-to-read face, luminous dial. Has outside locking bezel, which can be set as a lapsed time for Estimated Time of Arrival, or for various time zones.
7650.

CHRONOMAT — 17 Jewel, Exclusive Slide Rule, Chronograph; solves complicated mathematical and engineering problems: multiplication, division, ratios, interest, percentages, speeds, averages, etc.
7691 Stainless steel.

7692 Gold filled.

7693 18 Kt. gold.

UNITIME — 17 Jewel, automatic self-winding, exclusive wristwatch, featuring the date, and indicating the time at 24 capitals of World's time zones. Indispensable for the international businessman.
1260 Stainless steel.

1261 Gold filled.

transOcean

civilian version of the watch that has won the confidence of professional fliers. For men and for ladies - two highly exclusive models, both automatic, and both identified by the engraving on the case back which illustrates Breitling's participation in world aviation.

The TransOcean, equipped with an amazingly accurate movement — completely automatic, shock protected, antimagnetic — housed in a superwaterproof case.

For men (with calendar)
1001 Steel.

1002 Gold top.

1003 18 Kt. gold.

For ladies
2001 Steel.

2002 Gold top.

2003 18 Kt. gold.

superOcean

The new SuperOcean 20 atmos. (600 ft.) was specially created for deep sea exploration and to cater for the fast growing popularity of underwater sports.

807 Chronograph with time-out feature, revolving bezel, all stainless steel case, bright luminous dial, 30 minute chronographic recorder ensuring accurate submersion timing. Adjustable steel mesh bracelet.

1004 Automatic watch (fully self-winding). Revolving bezel ensures complete protection of the safety glass crystal and easy underwater manipulation, even with gloved fingers. Adjustable steel mesh bracelet.

Opposite page: American Breitling advertisement, circa 1970, showing watches that had already been on the market for some years. Top: $400-450; Center: $2200-2500 GF: $3000-3500 18 Kt., $2000-2500, $2000-2200 GF: $30003500 18Kt., $2500-2800 SS: 2500-2800 GF; Bottom row: $250-300 for men, $150-200 for ladies, $450-600 GF.: $1100-1500, $1100-1500.

Élégance 1914

G. LÉON Breitling S.A.

LA CHAUX-DE-FONDS . SUISSE

Various advertisements from the forties, especially for ladies' watches. Center right: $175-225 ea.; Bottom: $600-800, $600-800.

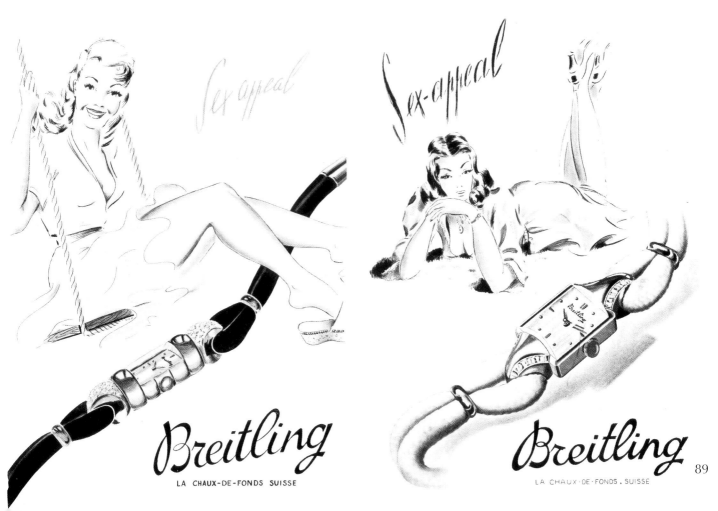

Sex-appeal

Sex-appeal

Breitling

LA CHAUX-DE-FONDS SUISSE

Breitling

LA CHAUX-DE-FONDS . SUISSE

89

Watches With Chronometer Certificates

A watch may be called a "chronometer" if it has passed an accuracy test and attains a certain level of accuracy regarding timekeeping. The "chronometer" definition was accepted by the Association of Swiss Watch Factories in 1939 and revised in 1951, when the term for position testing was added. The tests were carried out by the official offices for watch accuracy testing, which have been located since their origin in 1900 at La Chaux-de-Fonds, Le Locle, Biel, Saint Imier and Le Sentier, or by observatories in Geneva and Neuenburg. These agencies then issue the accuracy certificates for the tested watches.

Testing is carried out in five different positions and at three different temperatures, lasting a total of fifteen days. The various positions and temperatures are intended to simulate being worn on a person's wrist, which is most likely how the watch will be used. Good results include variations of no more than -1 and +10 seconds per day. These results can be attained by precise adjustment and optimal balance of a watch. Although these watches have not been tested officially, and therefore cannot officially be called "chronometers", many watches made by Breitling are so well adjusted that chronometer precision is actually attained by them anyway.

Advertising for watches with "Chronometer Certificate", circa 1965. $800-1000, $800-900, $300-400.

CHRONOMETER

 BREITLING

DIE TRAUMUHR

Auf dem einzigartig . Vertrauensverhältnis mit der Weltluftfahrt ist eine weitere Schöpfung Breitlings – die automatische TransOcean – aufgebaut. Das Herz der TransOcean ist ein vollautomatisches, stoßsicheres und antimagnetisches 25-Rubine-Werk von erstaunlicher Gangtreue. Der große und kräftige Ro-

tor der Automatvorrichtung ist in einem besonders widerstandsfähigen Lager eingesetzt. Er ist mit einem schweren Metallkranz versehen, was einen sicheren Aufzug gewährleistet. Die TransOcean ist dank dem Durchmesser der Unruhe Glucydur außergewöhnlich präzis reguliert. Das Ganze umgibt ein höchst dichtes Gehäuse, in dessen Boden ein Echtheitszeichen eingraviert ist, welches Breitlings Zugehörigkeit zur Welt der Flieger bezeugt. In einem Wort: ein wertvoller, selten schöner Zeitmesser!

Mod. TO-3 ohne Datum
Crocoband DM **980.-** *
Mod. TO-4 mit Datum
Crocoband DM **999.-** *

Gold »CHRONOMETER«
die vollkommenste Schöpfung aus unserer Kollektion ... automatische TransOcean in Chronometerausführung, amtlich geprüft, mit offiziellem Gangschein, schwerem wasserdichtem 18karätigem Goldgehäuse, Ziffern aus Gold, auf wunderschönem, mattversilbertem Zifferblatt. In Croco-Luxus-Geschenkschatulle.

Stahl »CHRONOMETER«
Automatische TransOcean in Chronometerausführung, amtlich geprüft, mit offiziellem Gangschein, elegantes wasserdichtes Edelstahlgehäuse, mattversilbertes Zifferblatt mit echten Weißgoldstrichen, Datumfenster, in Luxusschatulle mit schmiegsamem verstellbarem Edelstahlarmband
Mod. TO-8   DM **525.-** *

* Unverbindlicher Richtpreis

Breitling ist Lieferant der Armee, Marine und Luftwaffe der USA

"Trans-Ocean" chronometer, circa 1968 (upper left). $200-250

American advertising for chronometers (below). SS: $300-400, SSw/bracelet: $400-500, Gold: $400-500; $400-500, waterproof: $400-500, Navitimer: $1100-1200.

Watches with running certificates, from the 1953 catalog. Top to bottom: $750-950, $750-950, $750-950, $750-850, $800-1000, $900-1000.

BREITLING
GENEVA

─*transOcean*

A splendid inspiration, a truly magnificent watch. Movement of unerring precision. Waterproof & fully Automatic

Stainless steel	£44. 0.0.
Stainless steel with bracelet	£47. 0.0.
Gold capped	£50.15.0.

Other conventional Models from £16.19.6.

THE CHRONOMAT

Solves your mathematical problems simply & speedily
£35.10.0.

Waterproof chronograph
£37.0.0.
Navitimer £42.0.0.

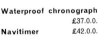

SOLE AGENT IN UNITED KINGDOM
W.WRIGHT Ltd THE JEWELLERS
529, Oxford Street (Marble Arch), London W.1 & Provinces
Post Enquiries - 7, Stone Street, Brighton 1

Breitling

DE LA QUALITÉ EN SÉRIE
QUALITY PRODUCED IN SERIES
QUALITÄT IN SERIEN

Chronographs

The term "chronograph" generally denotes a watch that, in addition to normal time measurement, allows measurements of amounts of elapsed time, which is indicated on auxiliary dials. To do this, a chronograph is equipped with a start-stop mechanism with which one can start a separate timing mechanism and stop it and reset it to zero at any chosen time. There is a great variety of functions. Seconds, minutes and seconds, even hours, minutes and seconds can be measured. Operating the chronograph will not interfere with normal running of the watch.

Chronographs have always had top priority at Breitling, for the good reason that these products have been very successful. Just think of the chronographs of the thirties, the Chronomat of the forties, and even the Chronomat-Chrono-Matic of the sixties.

Let us take the Chronomat-Chrono-Matic as an example of the operation that is customary for most chronographs. The Chrono-Matic has two buttons, one by the 2 and the other by the 4. The one by the 2 operates the starting and stopping mechanism. It can be started and stopped as often as desired, and the total time then added up. The button by the 4 is used only to set the counter back to the zero position. There are also other chronographs in which the button by the 2 is used only for starting. The button by the 4 is then used for both stopping and zero setting. These functions depend on the movement design, but the majority are as described here.

Advertising for the chronograph with the armband and a second button (Breitling patent); until then it was customary to control the functions with one button; circa 1934. $2200-2500

Fitted with a variety of dials, chronographs perform varied tasks. The scales on the dials are often made to event requirements to compare with elapsed time. One can read a patient's pulse rate directly from a chronograph made for physicians by comparing where the sweep hand stops at the graduated scale. This scale often goes up to 15 pulsations. On a telemetric scale, one can see directly, for example, how far away a storm is by comparing the sweep hand position with the outside scale. If the chronograph is started when lightning is seen and stopped when thunder is heard, the sweep hand points to the distance (in kilometers or miles) from the lightning source. A further possibility is the measurement of speed. Based on a certain distance, the chronograph is started at the beginning of the ride and stopped after the distance is completed, allowing the average speed to be read directly. Many different chronographs for the varied tasks are available on the market.

The unique feature of the Chronomat-Chrono-Matic is its construction. The chronograph consists of a basic movement unit and a chrono-section unit. These two units are attached with screws, one on top of the other. The design required that the winding stem with the crown had to be moved to the position of the 9, at first what seems like a surprising innovation that all firms agreed would be the best. Since obviously this watch does not often need to be wound up by hand, then it follows that the chronograph buttons would be better located on the right side of the case.

Since this chronograph is an automatic one, a suitable winding mechanism is required. The heavy microrotor that winds the mainspring is housed in the basic movement and has a pointed dead angle of only 11 degrees, which means that even relatively inactive wearers can always depend on the watch being wound up. (The dead angle is the portion of the rotating movement in which the spring is not wound.) The rotor arrangement is patented, just as is the mechanical equalizer that transfers the movements of the rotor through a gear to the mainspring in the form of winding power.

In addition, a special regulator setting was developed for this watch, with eccentric setting and moveable spiral block, which allow precise regulation and smallest error in the timing. These developments are also patented. The mechanical attachment of the two units of the movement is done, as already noted, by three screws. The coupling of the basic movement with the chrono-section was effected by a swinging drive

G. LÉON BREITLING S.A., MONTBRILLANT WATCH MY., LA CHAUX-DE-FONDS (SUISSE)

NOUVEAUTÉ

LE SEUL
CHRONOGRAPHE-COMPTEUR BRACELET
À DEUX POUSSOIRS
OFFRANT

POUR TOUS LES SPORTS
FOOT-BALL ETC.

POUR L'INDUSTRIE

UN MAXIMUM
D'AVANTAGES
D'UTILITÉ, ET
DE PERFECTION

N° 100
CHRONOGRAPHE-COMPTEUR 16'''
QUALITÉ SOIGNÉE
,, BREVETÉ''

SYSTÈMES BREVETÉS SUR CALIBRES 14''', 14½''', 15''', 15½''' & 16'''
CHRONOGRAPHE-COMPTEUR BRACELET PERMETTANT LE CALCUL EFFECTIF DU TEMPS DE TOUTES OBSERVATIONS
ARRÊT FACULTATIF DE LA GRANDE TROTTEUSE   REMISE A ZÉRO INDÉPENDANTE   PEUT SE LIVRER AVEC COMPTEUR 45 MINUTES

coupling. When the chronograph is started, the swinging drive is brought into contact with the second-counting wheel of the chronograph by means of a rocker. When stopped, the swinging drive swings out and the second-counting wheel is blocked by a brake.

Exploded view of Breitling Caliber 11 automatic movement, with the chrono-section removed.

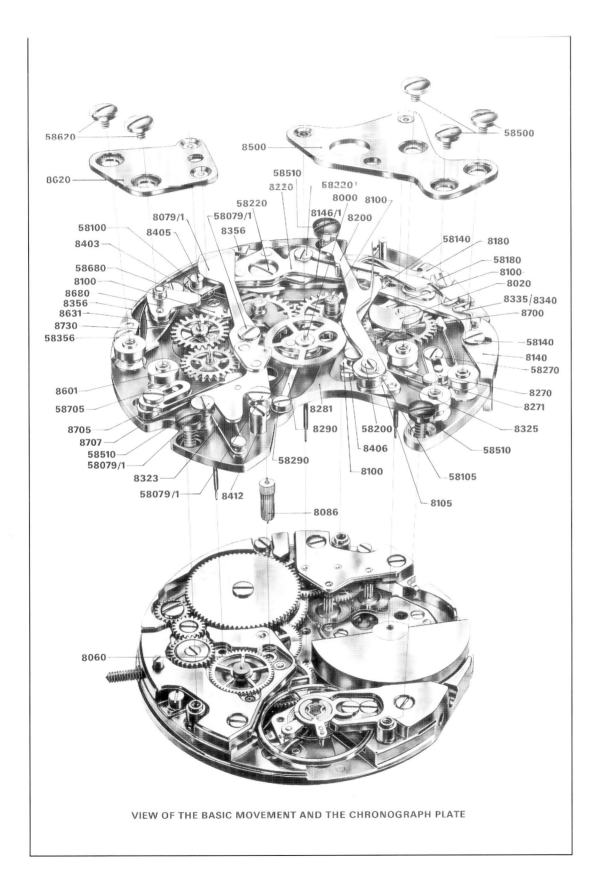

VIEW OF THE BASIC MOVEMENT AND THE CHRONOGRAPH PLATE

Since it was possible to locate the drive for the hour counter in the basic movement, the result was the first chronograph with an hour counter, date and automatic winding, and all this without a columnar wheel.

The quick switching of the date, along with the turning ring of the bezel, were also patented, and several additional patents concern the chrono-section. The functioning of the individual elements is shown in the exploded drawings below.

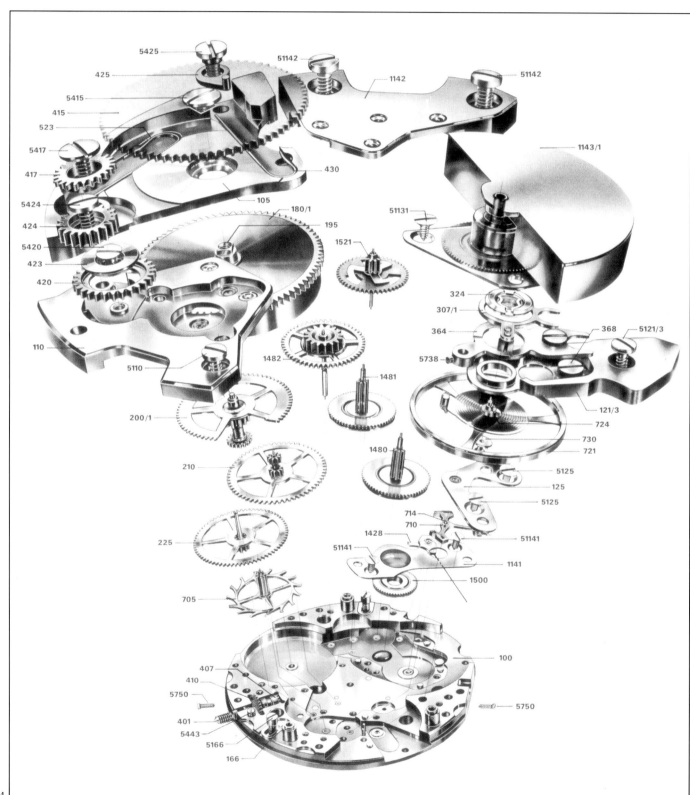

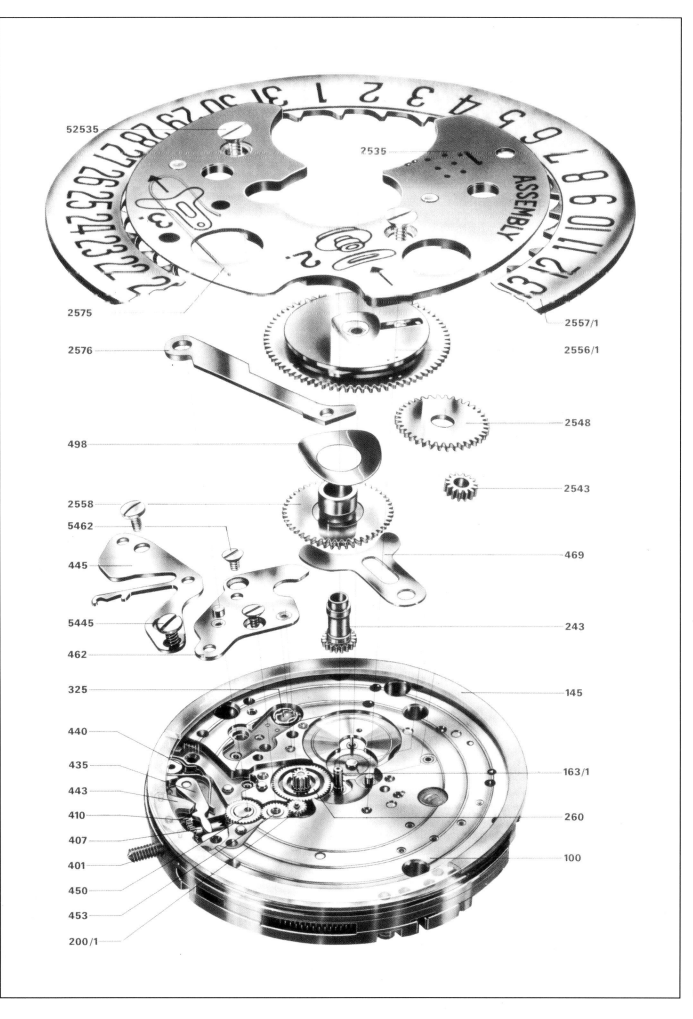

The patented bezel-turning mechanism of the Chrono-Matic series

Cutaway of the waterproof case with the turning inner ring

1. Middle section of case
2. Outer turning ring
3. Bottom
4. O-ring seal for bottom
5. Housing
6. Glass
7. Tension ring
8. Spring for turning ring
9. Inside turning ring
10. Outer shell
11. External drive
12. Internal drive
12. O-ring seals
14. Case ring

To remove the component composed of parts 10, 11 and 12:
a. Remove the black housing 5 with a lever.
b. Hold the drive 11 firmly and unscrew the drive 12.
c. After replacing the component, drive the housing 5 all the way in, to guarantee the watertightness of the case.

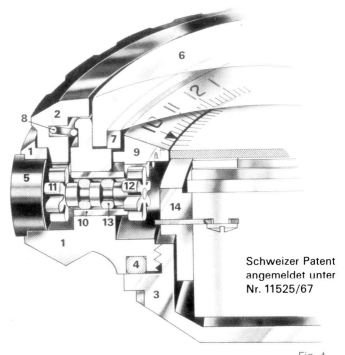

Schweizer Patent angemeldet unter Nr. 11525/67

Fig. 4

Drawing of the swinging-drive coupling (left)

The play-free hand mechanism (right)

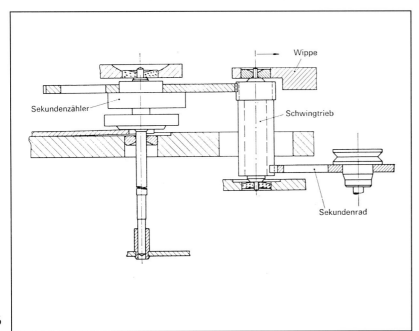

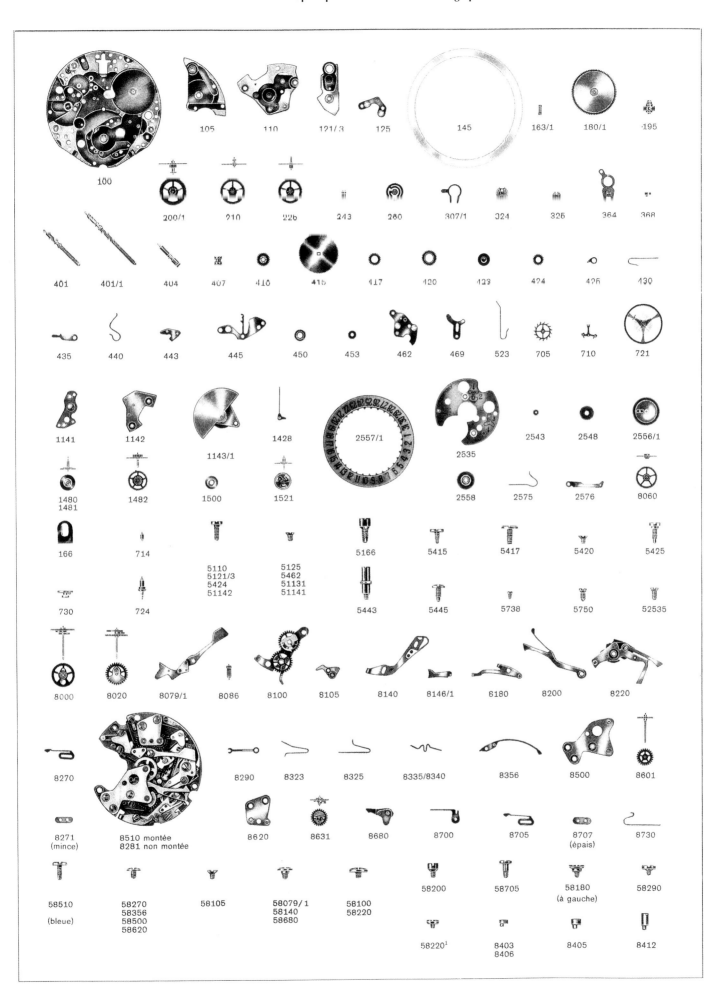

100

105 110 121/3 125 145 163/1 180/1 195

200/1 210 225 243 280 307/1 324 325 364 368

401 401/1 404 407 416 415 417 420 423 424 425 430

435 440 443 445 450 453 462 469 523 705 710 721

1141 1142 1143/1 1428 2557/1 2535 2543 2548 2556/1

1480
1481 1482 1500 1521 2558 2575 2576 8060

166 714 5166 5415 5417 5420 5425

5110
5121/3
5424
51142

5125
5462
51131
51141

730 724 5443 5445 5738 5750 52535

8000 8020 8079/1 8086 8100 8105 8140 8146/1 8180 8200 8220

8270 8290 8323 8325 8335/8340 8356 8500 8601

8271
(mince)

8510 montée
8281 non montée

8620 8631 8680 8700 8705 8707
(épais) 8730

58510

(bleue)

58270
58356
58500
58620

58105 58079/1
58140
58680

58100
58220

58200 58705 58180
(à gauche) 58290

58220[1] 8403
8406 8405 8412

97

Öffnen Sie Ihr Schaufenster ins XXI. Jahrhundert!

mit dem automatischen Chronograph

Sie werden all Ihre alten Kunden wiedersehen, die von ihrem Navitimer... Chronomat... Top Time usw. ... so begeistert sind, dass sie ihn sofort in der Chrono - matic-Ausführung besitzen werden wollen – nämlich automatisch.

Sie werden eine neue Käuferschicht in Ihr Geschäft strömen sehen, die Ihren Ruf noch weiterverbreitet. Denn Sie haben das Produkt in der Hand, das es noch nirgends gab und das so oft verlangt wurde.

Jetzt hat niemand mehr die Qual der Wahl: automatische Uhr oder Chronograph? Der Chronomatic Breitling vereinigt beide!

The Chronomat-Chrono-Matic series of 1969 at a glance. Clockwise: $600-750, $500-600, $200-300, $500-600, $500-650, $700-800, $800-900, $800-900.

Chrono-matic

BREITLING GENÈVE

G. Léon Breitling S.A.
Rue Adrien Lachenal 26, Genève, Suisse

98

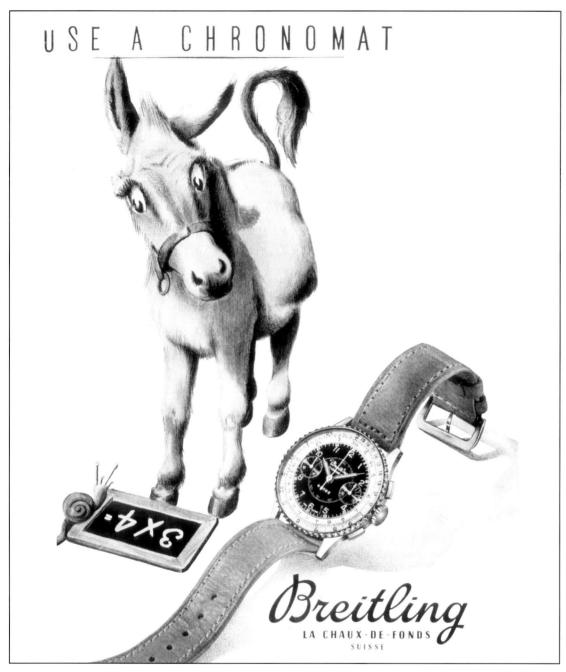

USE A CHRONOMAT

Breitling
LA CHAUX-DE-FONDS
SUISSE

Advertisement for the Chronomat, circa 1946. $3000-3200

Advertisement for the "Datora" with calendar, circa 1952. $2000-2200

Breitling "Duograph" chronograph with sweep hand, circa
1944, with patented push-button
function in the crown. $1800-2000

Pointing out the functions of the
Chronomat, circa 1942. $3500-4000

Breitling "Premier", circa 1948. $900-1000 ea.

Chronograph, circa 1942 (left). $900-1000

"Trans-Ocean, circa 1972 (center). $600-700

"Datora", circa 1968 (right). $600-700

"Sprint", circa 1969. $600-800 ea.

"Unitime" with 24-hour dial, circa 1965 (left). $500-650

"Sprint", circa 1968 (right). $500-650

"Chronomat-Chrono-Matic", circa 1970 (left). $1200-1500

"Long Playing", circa 1974 (center). $800-900

Referee's watch, circa 1972 (right). $500-600

Chronograph, circa 1944 (left). $800-900

Chronograph with springing minute indication in the chrono-section, circa 1960. $600-800

"Duograph" chronograph with sweep hand, stopped via the crown, circa 1952. $1200-1500

Chronomat with calendar and moon phase, plus sweep-hand function, circa 1950. $5000-6000

"Unitime" automatic with world-time indication, circa 1970 (left). $1000-1100

Chronograph with "LB" (Leon Breitling) signature, circa 1946 (right). $900-1000

"Duograph" with sweep hand and calendar, circa 1952.
$4500-5000

"Chronomat" in revised form, circa 1945. $4500-5000

COMPASS

In every realm of technology, equipment is now extremely costly and highly sophisticated. But if your timing is out, sometimes by only a split second, even the most advanced technology may become completely useless. The watch is the nerve centre of the equipment, the key to the success of the operation. The BREITLING COMPASS WATCH is built to the most exacting military and scientific requirements. Waterproof to 300 ft. and capable of withstanding severe climatic conditions (−20° to +50°), it is an all-purpose instrument for night and day, designed for diving, rescue operations and underwater maintenance work.

Shown on the mirror base of the compass: distress signals. On the patented data-code strap: graduated scales (decimetre and feet) and morse code.

Breitling "Compass", circa 1986. $500-600

Chronographs from the 1946 catalog. Top left: $2400-2600 ea.; Top right: $1200-1500; Bottom left: $12-1500. $1800-2000; Bottom right, $2000-2200.

"Cosmonaute" in a small case, circa 1968. $4000-4500

"Top Time", circa 1968 (lower left). $1500-1800

Chronograph from the 1953 catalog. $3000-3500

"Long Playing", circa 1970 $1800-2000

Chronographs from the big 1953 catalog. Top row: $800-1000 ea.; Center row: $1200-1500. $1200-1500. $1000-1200. $1000-1200.; Bottom row: Top: $1200-1500. $900-1000. Center: $1000-1100. $1200-1500. Bottom: $650-700. $1100-1200.

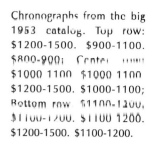

Chronographs from the big 1953 catalog. Top row: $1200-1500. $900-1100. $800-900; Center row: $1000-1100. $1000-1100. $1200-1500. $1000-1100; Bottom row: $1100-1200. $1100-1200. $1100-1200. $1200-1500. $1100-1200.

Spare parts for chronographs
from 10.5 to 14 lignes

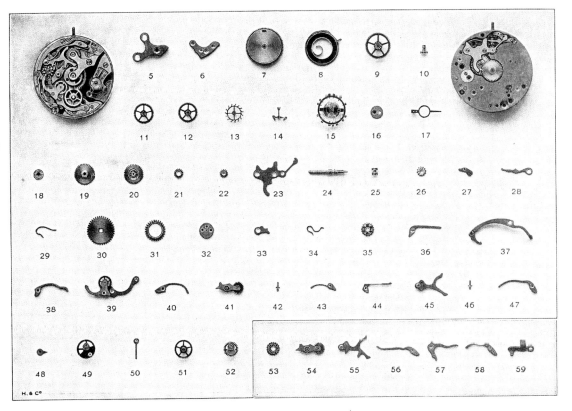

RÉF. 10 ½ ''' 101   POUR CHRONOGRAPHES
FOR CHRONOGRAPHS   Nos   727 - 728 - 729 - 753
FÜR DIE CHRONOGRAPHEN   754 - 755 - 756

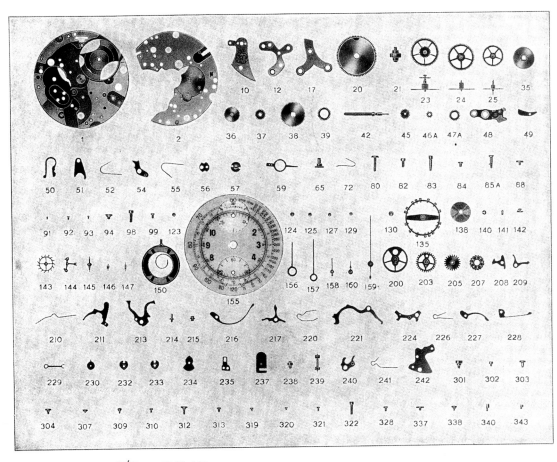

RÉF. 12 ½ ''' 103

POUR CHRONOGRAPHES
FOR CHRONOGRAPHS   Nos   170 - 171 - 172 - 173 - 174
FÜR DIE CHRONOGRAPHEN   175 - 176 - 177 - 178 - 179

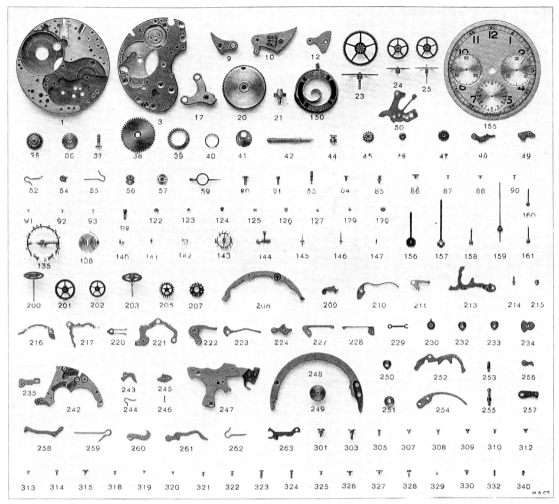

Spare parts for chronographs from 10.5 to 14 lignes

RÉF. 13-14''' 105

POUR CHRONOGRAPHES
FOR CHRONOGRAPHS Nos
FÜR DIE CHRONOGRAPHEN

701 - 710 - 734 - 737 - 747 - 760 - 765 - 767 - 769 - 771
772 - 773 - 774 - 775 - 776 - 777 - 778 - 779 - 780 - 781
782 - 789 - 790 - 621 - 622 - 623 - 629 - 641 - 642

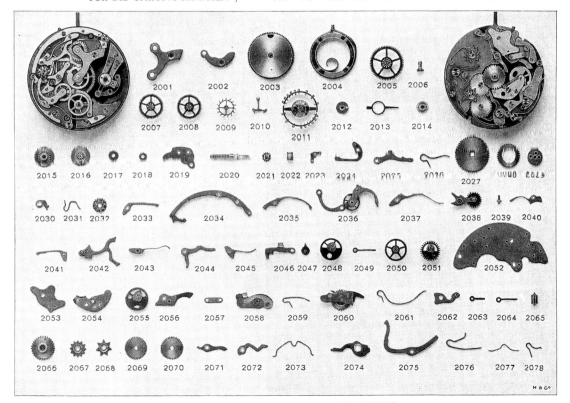

RÉF. 14''' 107 Datora

POUR CHRONOGRAPHES
FOR CHRONOGRAPHS Nos 784 - 785
FÜR DIE CHRONOGRAPHEN

"Navitimer", circa 1965 (above). $2500-3000

"Pult" with automatic movement, circa 1971 (below). $1100-1200

"Chrono-Matic", circa 1970 (above). $3200-3500

"Chronomat", circa 1970 (below). $3000-3200

"Datora", circa 1968 (above). $800-900

"Long Playing", circa 1968 (below). $800-1000

"Long Playing", circa 1970 (above). $800-900

"Chrono-Matic", circa 1972 (below). $800-1000

"GMT" with automatic movement, circa 1970 (above). $1000-1100

"Datora", circa 1968 (below). $900-1000

"Sprint", circa 1970. $750-900

"Cosmonaute", hand-wound, circa 1968 (left). $2000-2200

"Co-Pilot", hand-wound, circa 1968 (right). $600-700

Nicht automatisch
wasserdicht
12-Stundenzähler
819 Stahl

Nicht automatisch
wasserdicht
12-Stundenzähler
7650 Stahl

"GMT", hand-wound, circa 1968 (left). $1200-1500

Breitling table clock, circa 1965 (right). $600-700

Nicht automatisch
wasserdicht
12-Stundenzähler
812 Stahl*

AVI

KLM

PAA

JAL

CONVAIR

UNITED
AIR LINES

EASTERN AIR LINES

B BREITLING
GENÈVE
Im Dienste der Weltluftfahrt

VICKERS B·O·A·C LOCKHEED
AIRCRAFT CORPORATION

NAVITIMER

Advertising for chrono
graphs, circa 1950. Top:
$1500-1800. $3000-3200.;
Center: $900-1000. $1000-
1100. $1000-1100 ; Bot-
tom: $900-1000 ea.

760 (= ⌀ 35 mm)
789 (= ⌀ 33 mm)
ab Fr. 189.-
Kleine Sekunde, Se-
kunde aus der Mitte,
45-Minuten-Totalisa-
tor, Tachometer.

734 (= ⌀ 37 mm)
787 (= ⌀ 35 mm)
ab Fr. 218.-
Kleine Sekunde, Sekunde aus der Mitte, 30-
Minuten-Totalisator, spezieller 12-Stunden-To-
talisator, Tachometer.

765 wasserdicht
(= ⌀ 38 mm)

788 wasserdicht
(= ⌀ 36 mm)

ab Fr. 248.-

2100
ab Fr. 137.-

1191
wasserdicht
ab Fr. 170.-

1190
ab Fr. 137.-

Kleine Sekunde, Sekunde aus der Mitte, 45-Minuten-Totalisator, Tachometer und
Telemeter. Stossgesicnert, antimagnetisch, 17 Steine.

119

IHR
PERSÖNLICHES
BORDINSTRUMENT

Einen BREITLING NAVITIMER zu tragen ist etwas völlig anderes als nur eine sehr schöne Uhr sein eigen zu nennen.

Denn nichts ist mit dem NAVITIMER zu vergleichen. Von allen Chronographen ist er derjenige, welcher mit einem Bordinstrument die größte Ähnlichkeit hat.

Der BREITLING NAVITIMER hat das imposante Aussehen eines Hochleistungs- und Wettkampfzeitmessers. Und dies erklärt sich durch seinen Ursprung, seinen Werdegang**:

Der NAVITIMER wurde mit dem Aufschwung der zivilen Luftfahrt geboren. Er hat sich deshalb alle Funktionen zu eigen gemacht, die ihn mit der Aeronautik verbinden. Die Gewähr hierfür ist das totale Vertrauen der Luftfahrt in den NAVITIMER – für diesen Präzisionschronographen gleicht dies dem Diplom eines Co-Piloten.

Wohlgemerkt, der BREITLING NAVITIMER ist nicht ausschließlich den Piloten des Linienflugs oder den Besitzern von Privatmaschinen vorbehalten. Auch Rallyefahrer, Sportler und Intellektuelle mit ausgesprochen dynamischem Lebensstil haben ihn zu schätzen gelernt.

Seit über 20 Jahren schon findet man den BREITLING NAVITIMER in stetig zunehmender Zahl am Arm von prominenten Persönlichkeiten, die nicht unbedingt der Welt des Sports oder der Technik angehören. Sein Stil ist – wie der eines Rolls Royce – zeitlos: mechanische Perfektion und die Vollkommenheit seiner Ausführung haben nun den Punkt der Vollendung erreicht. Es ist der NAVITIMER.

** Breitling hat sich seit 1884 (dem Geburtsjahr des Automobils) der Fabrikation von Spezial-Stoppuhren eigener Erfindung und Chronographen gewidmet. Seit 1936 hat er sich durch seinen Bordchronographen einen Namen im Bereich der Luftfahrt gemacht. Und im Jahre 1969 brachte BREITLING den ersten automatischen Chronographen auf den Markt. Diese Schweizer Fabrik – auch heute noch ein Familienbetrieb – hat auf ihrem Gebiet den Rang einer Weltmarke erreicht und nimmt intensiv an der Beschleunigung des technischen Fortschritts in der Messung kurzer Zeiten teil: ihr Zeuge – der NAVITIMER

AN "INTELLIGENT" INSTRUMENT: THE NAVITIMER

The "watch" is passive, but the chronograph is active.

1 Logarithmic scales of an aviation computer—the one fixed, the other turnable

2 30-minute and 12-hour counters

3 Date indication

"Navitimer" instructions $1800-2000

INSTRUCTIONS FOR THE USE OF THE BREITLING NAVITIMER

The Navitimer is equipped with the logarithmic scales of a slide rule. We have chosen the position of the moveable outer scale in order to allow for the calculatory processes described here. Of course, as with any calculator, one must first keep in mind the decimal place. These are only a few simple examples among the countless calculating operations in the instructions for use, which are delivered with every NAVITIMER.

Multiplication:
Multiplier 3 (white scale) must be set at the number 10 of the black scale, so that all numbers on the black scale automatically are multiplied by the 3 on the white scale, thus:
3 x 5 = 15
3 x 4 = 12
3 x 15 = 45 etc.

Division:
The scales are to be read in the opposite direction. The numbers of the white scale are automatically divided by 3; the result can be read on the white scale opposite the number 10, thus:
15 / 5 = 3
12 / 4 = 3
75/ 25 = 3

Calculation of speed per hour:
9 km (on the white scale) driven in the time of 3 minutes (on the black scale). The result can be read on the white scale opposite the MPH marking: 180 km per hour. In the same way, 45 km (white scale) in 15 minutes (black scale) = 180 kph (white scale opposite the MPH marking).

Distance covered in a given time and at a specified speed: At 180 kph (MPH marking) in 1 hour and 10 minutes (1:10 on the inner black scale), one gets the result as 210 km (on the white scale).

The time needed to cover a certain distance at a certain speed: At a speed of 180 kph (MPH marking), to cover 270 km (white scale), it would take 1 hour and 30 minutes (1:30 on the black inner scale)

121

Mod. 816/14
Der bewährte NAVITIMER mit Handaufzug, fabrikseitig auf 5 atü Wasserdichte geprütes Edelstahlgehäuse, Edelstahlband. 30-Minuten- und 12-Stundenzähler.

Mod. 7806-S
Der klassische NAVITIMER mit Handaufzug im „kleinen" nichtwasserdichten Edelstahlgehäuse. 30-Minuten- und 12-Stundenzähler sowie Datum.
Auf Wunsch auch mit Stahlband.

Mod. 1809/14
NAVITIMER CHRONO-MATIC mit automatischem Aufzug. Alle Eigenschaften des Modells 1806/14, jedoch in „Überschall"-Ausführung mit 24-Stunden-Zifferblatt.

Mod. 1806/14
NAVITIMER CHRONO-MATIC mit automatischem Aufzug. Robustes Edelstahlgehäuse, fabrikseitig auf 5 atü Wasserdichte geprüft, Edelstahlband, 30-Minuten- und 12-Stundenzähler, Datum.

Modell 8806
NAVITIMER CHRONO-MATIC mit automatischem Aufzug und dem klassischen „kleineren" nichtwasser- dichten Edelstahlgehäuse. Ebenfalls 30-Minuten- und 12-Stundenzähler, Datum, Lederband.

Mod. 8806/5
dto. in Massivgold 18 Karat.

Top left: $2500-3000. $2200-2500.; Top right: $3000-3200. $3200-3800. $3000-3200; Bottom right: $100-150 ea.

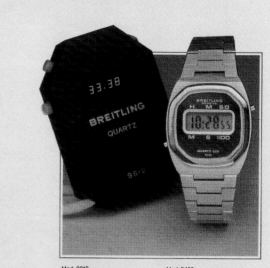

Mod. 9612
BREITLING-Genf bietet mit dieser sensationellen LED-Quartz-Stoppuhr nicht nur einen Chrono- graphen mit Langzeitstoppung (max. 99 Stunden, 59 Minuten, 59 Sekunden, 99 Hundertstel- sekunden), Split-Time, Lap-Time. Diese Stoppuhr zeigt auf Knopf- druck auch die normale Tageszeit (Stunde, Minute, Sekunde, Tag, Monat und Wochentag) mit aller- größter Präzision. Mattschwarzes Metallgehäuse mit praktischer Umhängekordel. Ein perfektes Zeitmeßgerät.

Mod. 9403
Ein superflacher LCD-Quartz- Chronograph mit höchster Präzision. Daueranzeige von Stunde, Minute, Sekunde, zusätz- lich Datum und Monat. Auf Knopf- druck Beleuchtung sowie unabhängig von der Uhrzeit laufendes Chronographen-Stopp- werk, Anzeige bis 59 Minuten, 59 Sekunden und 99 Hundertstel- sekunden. Split-Time und Lap-Time. Elegantes Edelstahlgehäuse, fabrikseitig auf 4 atü geprüft, integriertes kürzbares Edelstahl- band. Zifferblatteinfassung blau wie Abbildung oder auch silber- farbig im Charakter des Stahl- bandes.

DER BREITLING NAVITIMER JETZT AUCH IN QUARTZ-AUSFÜHRUNG

Die Elektronik hat durch die Einführung des Quarzwerkes eine organische Revolution in der Entwicklung der Uhr eingeleitet.

Deshalb präsentiert Ihnen BREITLING den NAVITIMER auch in Quartz-Ausführung, und zwar in den beiden Versionen: LED und LCD.

Der NAVITIMER bewahrt auf diese Weise all seine Funktionen als Zeitmesser mit logarithmischen Skalen. Er ist ein mechanisches Werkzeug, welches den Gedankengängen desjenigen folgt, der sich seiner zum Rechnen bedient. Aber zugleich wurde eine Zahlenanzeige mit Speicherung eingeführt, welche erst durch die elektronische Zeitmessung entstand.

Auf der Anzeige erscheinen, je nach Wunsch, Stunden, Minuten, Sekunden, das Datum mit automatischer Kalenderanpassung und die Angabe jeglicher Stoppuhr-Messungen (1/100 Sekunden).

Dieses BREITLING-Konzept ist eine bemerkenswerte Kombination des Gebrauchs logarithmischer Skalen und elektronischer Zeitmessung.

Mod. 0400
Der klassische NAVITIMER im „kleineren" nichtwasserdichten Edelstahlgehäuse mit LCD-Quartz-System. Daueranzeige von Stunde, Minute, Sekunde, zusätzlich Datum und Monat.
Auf Knopfdruck Beleuchtung sowie unabhängig von der Uhrzeit laufendes Chronographen-Stoppwerk, Anzeige bis 59 Minuten, 59 Sekunden und 99 Hundertstelsekunden, Split-Time und Lap-Time. Auf Wunsch auch mit Edelstahlband.

Mod. 9106
Der NAVITIMER mit LED-Quartz-System. Anzeige von 15 verschiedenen Funktionen auf Knopfdruck, Stunden, Minuten, Sekunden, Datum, Wochentag, Monat sowie alle Funktionen eines komplizierten Additionschronographen.
Unabhängig von der normalen Uhrzeit laufendes Chronographen-Stoppwerk mit Möglichkeit der Langzeitstoppung bis 99 Stunden, 59 Minuten, 59 Sekunden und 99 Hundertstelsekunden. Die perfekte Elektronik erlaubt auch das Speichern und Addieren gestoppter Zeiten und Zwischenablesung der Uhrzeit, des Datums etc.
Leichte Ablesbarkeit, auch bei Nacht, dank Leuchtdiodenanzeige. Die beiden Mini-Knopfbatterien sind leicht auswechselbar und sorgen für größte Ganggenauigkeit. Edelstahlgehäuse, fabrikseitig auf 5 atü Wasserdichte geprüft, Edelstahlband.

Mod. 9416
Der NAVITIMER im „großen" Gehäuse mit LCD-Quartz-System. Wie alle NAVITIMER mit der logarithmischen Skala für alle Rechenarten. Daueranzeige von Stunde, Minute, Sekunde, zusätzlich Datum und Monat. Auf Knopfdruck Beleuchtung sowie unabhängig von der Uhrzeit laufendes Chronographen-Stoppwerk, Anzeige bis 59 Minuten, 59 Sekunden und 99 Hundertstelsekunden, Split-Time und Lap-Time. Edelstahlgehäuse, fabrikseitig auf 5 atü Wasserdichte geprüft, Edelstahlband.

Various chronographs from the 1974 catalog. Top right: $400-500. $500-600.; Bottom left: $500-600.

BREITLING
GENÈVE

NAVITIMER
COSMONAUTE

Official Timepiece of the Aircraft
Owners' and Pilots' Association
(A.O.P.A.)

GEBRAUCHS-
ANWEISUNG
DES
CHRONOGRAPHEN
FÜR
PILOTEN
BREITLING-
NAVITIMER
UND COSMONAUTE

NAVITIMER

Ref. 806, nicht wasserdicht
Ref. 816, wasserdicht
Ref. 1806, wasserdicht, automatisch, Kalender

COSMONAUTE

Ref. 809, nicht wasserdicht
Ref. 819, wasserdicht
Ref. 1809, wasserdicht, automatisch, Kalender

INHALTS-
VERZEICHNIS

GEBRAUCHS-
ANWEISUNG

Der Navitimer ist ein Präzisionsinstrument, das dem Piloten, dem Funker, dem Navigator die Nützlichkeit eines Armbandchronographen, verbunden mit den logarithmischen Skalen eines Flugcomputers bietet.

Er gibt die genaue Zeit an, er totalisiert die Sekunden, Minuten und Stunden und seine beiden Drücker ermöglichen Unterbrechungen, wenn solche notwendig sein sollten. Es ist dem Piloten somit möglich, die effektive Flugzeit zusammenzuzählen, selbst bei mehreren Zwischenlandungen, indem er bei jeder Landung den Stoppzeiger anhält und beim Abflug wieder in Gang setzt. Der Minutenzähler (bei 3 Uhr) und der Stundenzähler (bei 6 Uhr) geben schlussendlich die totale Flugdauer an, die Zeit am Boden ist bereits ausgeschieden. Die Chronographenzeiger werden wie folgt beeinflusst: Ingangsetzen und Anhalten durch den oberen Drücker, Nullstellen durch den unteren Drücker.

Ist der Pilot mit der Anwendung des normalen Flugcomputers nicht vertraut, wird er etwas Zeit und Geduld brauchen, dieses Instrument beherrschen zu lernen. Es handelt sich um eine runde Rechenscheibe, anhand welcher Multiplikationen und Divisionen

5

---

zur Ermittlung der Zeit, der Distanz, des Brennstoffverbrauchs, der Geschwindigkeit und anderer, normaler Flugprobleme ausgeführt werden können. Betrachten wir den Navitimer: am äussersten Rand des Zifferblattes finden wir einen weissen Ring, der mit dem Glasring gedreht werden kann. Er trägt die Zahlen 10 — 10 (die Ziffer 10 kann ebenfalls 1, 10 oder 100 bedeuten). Wir nennen in dieser Gebrauchsanweisung diesen Ring die « weisse Skala ». Auf dem schwarzen Teil des Zifferblattes finden wir am äusseren Rand eine zweite Skala, die wir « schwarze Skala » nennen.

Es ist zu bemerken, dass die Ziffern der weissen Skala stets in Verbindung mit Meilen (oder km) oder Stundenmeilen, Fuss (oder Meter) oder Fuss (oder Meter) in der Minute, Gallons (oder Liter), oder Gallons (oder Liter) in der Stunde, oder einer anderen je nach der Zeit veränderlichen Menge steht. Auf der schwarzen Skala, bei 60 Min. finden wir einen Pfeil, markiert durch die Benennung MPH. Diese Bezeichnung ist das Merkzeichen für Stundengeschwindigkeiten oder für « Stunden ». Dieses Merkzeichen ist bei allen Problemen anzuwenden, die

mit einer Stundenquantität in Verbindung stehen (sei es in Meilen oder km).

Die schwarze Skala ist ausserdem mit einer weiteren, doppelten Zeitskala versehen, die die Umwandlung der Minuten gestattet, wenn das Total derselben die Stunde überschreitet: z.B. 70, 120, 450 auf dem äusseren schwarzen Ring der schwarzen Skala ergeben auf dem inneren Ring der schwarzen Skala: 1:10, 2:00, 7,5. (Die Ziffer 1:10 heisst: 1 Stunde 10 Minuten usw.)

6   7

RECHNUNGEN
AUF DER
GRUNDLAGE
EINES
NORMALEN
RECHEN-
SCHIEBERS

Sind Sie mit der Handhabung eines normalen Rechenschiebers vertraut, werden Sie feststellen, dass die weisse und die schwarze Skala den Skalen C und D des normalen Rechenschiebers gleichkommen. Multiplikationen, Divisionen und Dreisätze können somit auf die gleiche Weise gelöst werden. Sind Sie mit dem Rechenschieber nicht vertraut, merken Sie sich folgenden Grundsatz: Die Dezimale wird durch Schätzung festgelegt. Die Ziffer 10 kann also 1,0, 10, 100 oder 1 bedeuten. Bei einer Geschwindigkeitsberechnung, bei welcher das Resultat auf der Skala 15 ist, ist es klar, dass die Geschwindigkeit des Flugzeuges nicht 15, sondern 150 Stundenmeilen (oder Std./km) ist.

BEIM
MULTI-
PLIZIEREN

Beispiel 1

Beim Multiplizieren mit dem Navitimer wird das Einheitsmerkzeichen benützt. Ziffer 10 auf der äusseren schwarzen Skala. Der Multiplikator (Ziffer mit welcher eine andere Ziffer multipliziert wird) befindet sich auf der weissen Skala und wird dem Einheitsmerkzeichen auf der schwarzen Skala gegenüber gestellt. Das Resultat wird auf der weissen Skala, gegenüber dem Multiplikand (Ziffer die durch eine andere Ziffer multipliziert wird) abgelesen. (Der Multiplikand befindet sich auf der äusseren schwarzen Skala.)

Um 7×12 zu multiplizieren wird die Ziffer 12 (Multiplikator) auf der weissen Skala dem Merkzeichen « 10 » auf der schwarzen Skala gegenüber gestellt. Man liest gegenüber der Ziffer 7 (Multiplikand) der schwarzen Skala das Resultat: 84, auf der weissen Skala.

8   9

BEIM
DIVIDIEREN

Beispiel 2

Beim Dividieren mit dem Navitimer wird das gleiche Einheitsmerkzeichen benützt. Der Dividend (Quantität die durch eine Zahl geteilt wird) auf der weissen Skala wird dem Divisor (Zahl durch welche eine andere Zahl geteilt wird) auf der schwarzen Skala gegenüber gestellt. Das Resultat wird auf der weissen Skala, gegenüber dem Einheitsmerkzeichen (10 auf der schwarzen Skala) abgelesen.

Um 160 durch 4 zu dividieren, wird die Ziffer 16 der weissen Skala der

Ziffer 4 der schwarzen Skala gegenüber gestellt. Das Resultat: 40, wird auf der weissen Skala, gegenüber dem Einheitsmerkzeichen (10 auf der schwarzen Skala) abgelesen.

STUNDEN-
GESCHWINDIG-
KEIT

Die weisse und die schwarze Skala werden zur Berechnung der Stundengeschwindigkeiten benötigt. Zwei der nachstehenden Grössen sind bekannt: Zeitdauer, Distanz, Stundengeschwindigkeit.

Beispiel 3

Bekannt: Zeitdauer und Distanz.

Unbekannt: Stundengeschwindigkeit.

Ein Pilot stellt anhand von Merkpunkten fest,

dass er 104 Meilen (oder km) in 35 Minuten zurückgelegt hat. Welches ist seine Stundengeschwindigkeit?

LÖSUNG: Die Ziffer 104 der weissen Skala wird der Ziffer 35 der schwarzen Skala gegenüber gestellt. Gegenüber dem Stundenmerkzeichen

(Pfeil mit Benennung MPH bei 12 Uhr) wird das Resultat auf der weissen Skala abgelesen: 178 Meilen (oder km.) in der Stunde.

Beispiel 4

Bekannt: Distanz und Stundengeschwindigkeit.

Unbekannt: Zeitdauer.

10   11

Ein Pilot wünscht die Zeitdauer zu ermitteln, die er braucht, um eine Distanz von 486 Meilen (oder km) mit einer Stundengeschwindigkeit von 156 Meilen (oder km) zu durchfliegen.

LÖSUNG: Die Ziffer 156 auf der weissen Skala wird dem Stundenmerkzeichen (MPH) auf der schwarzen Skala gegenüber gestellt. Das Resultat ist auf der äusseren schwarzen Skala abzulesen gegenüber der Ziffer 486 auf der weissen Skala: 187 (oder 3 Stunden und 7 Minuten auf der inneren schwarzen Skala).

Beispiel 5

Bekannt: Zeitdauer und Geschwindigkeit.
Unbekannt: Distanz.
Ein Pilot wünscht die Distanz zu kennen, die er in 28 Minuten bei einer Stundengeschwindigkeit von 148 Meilen (oder km) durchfliegt.

LÖSUNG: Die Ziffer 148 der weissen Skala wird dem Stundenmerkzeichen (MPH) auf der schwarzen Skala gegenüber gestellt. Das Resultat ist auf der äusseren schwarzen Skala abzulesen. Geschwindigkeit dieselbe, ist es nicht mehr notwendig, die Skalen zu verschieben. Der Pilot kann somit ohne weiteres die durchflogene Distanz in 46 Minuten feststellen, indem er auf der weissen Skala gegenüber der Ziffer 46 der schwarzen Skala, die Distanz von 113 ½ Meilen (oder km) abliest.
Bemerkung: Bleibt die

MEILEN (oder km) IN DER MINUTE

Ist die Stundengeschwindigkeit in Meilen (oder km) bekannt, kann die Geschwindigkeit in der Minute festgestellt werden. Die Stundengeschwindigkeit, angegeben auf der weissen Skala und dem Stundenmerkzeichen MPH gegenüber gestellt, kann rasch in Meilen (oder km) in der Minute umgewandelt werden, indem das Resultat auf der

weissen Skala abgelesen wird gegenüber dem Einheitsmerkzeichen (10 auf der schwarzen Skala).

Beispiel 6

Im Beispiel 4 war die Stundengeschwindigkeit 156 Meilen (oder km). Die Ziffer 156 der weissen Skala war dem Stundenmerkzeichen MPH gegenüber gestellt. Welches ist die Geschwindigkeit in Meilen (oder km) per Minute?

LÖSUNG: Die Ziffer 156 der weissen Skala ist dem Stundenmerkzeichen gegenüber gestellt, das Resultat wird auf der weissen Skala gegenüber dem Einheitsmerkzeichen (10 auf der äusseren schwarzen Skala) abgelesen: 2,6 Meilen (oder km) in der Minute.

12 / 13

Es kann dem Piloten nutzbringend sein, die Zeitdauer einer kurzen Distanz zu kennen (z. B. Distanz zwischen zwei Punkten des Flughafens). In einem solchen Falle ist die Zeitdauer sehr kurz, weniger als eine Minute und es ist daher notwendig, die Ablesung in Sekunden vornehmen zu können. Wir benützen dafür das «Sekundenmerkzeichen», das durch die Ziffer 36 der äusseren schwarzen Skala dargestellt ist (es hat 3600 Sekunden in einer Stunde). Das folgende Beispiel erläutert dieses Problem.

Beispiel 7

Bekannt: Stundenmeilen (oder Std./km) und Distanz.
Unbekannt: Zeit in Sekunden um die Distanz zurückzulegen.
Ein Flugzeug nähert sich dem Flughafen mit einer Stundengeschwindigkeit von 120 Meilen (oder km). Die Distanz zwischen einem gewissen Punkt des Flughafens und dem Beginn der Piste ist 1 ½ Meilen (oder km). Der Pilot wünscht die Zeit zu kennen, die er braucht, um diese Distanz zu durchfliegen.

LÖSUNG: Die Ziffer 120 der weissen Skala wird dem Sekundenmerkzeichen gegenüber gestellt (Ziffer 36 der äusseren schwarzen Skala). Das Resultat ist auf der äusseren schwarzen Skala gegenüber der Ziffer 1,5 der weissen Skala abzulesen: 45 Sekunden.

BRENNSTOFF-VERBRAUCH

Zwei der nachstehenden Grössen sind bekannt, um den Brennstoffverbrauch zu berechnen: verbrauchte Quantität in Gallons (oder Liter), Zeit, Stundenverbrauch.

Beispiel 8

Bekannt: Zeit und Stundenverbrauch.
Unbekannt: Verbrauchte Quantität in Gallons (oder Liter).
Ein Pilot will wissen, wieviel Gallons (oder

Liter) notwendig sind, um 3 ½ Stunden fliegen zu können bei einem mittleren Stundenverbrauch von 11 ½ Gallons (oder Liter).

LÖSUNG: Die Ziffer 11,5 der weissen Skala wird dem Stundenmerkzeichen MPH gegenüber gestellt. Das Resultat

wird auf der weissen Skala abgelesen gegenüber der Ziffer 3 ½ Stunden auf der inneren schwarzen Skala (oder 210 Minuten auf der äusseren schwarzen Skala): 41 Gallons (oder Liter).

Beispiel 9

Bekannt: Die Quantität (Gallons oder Liter), der Stundenverbrauch.
Unbekannt: Zeit.
Ein Pilot hat 90 Gallons (oder Liter) zu seiner Verfügung. Für welche Zeit genügt diese Quantität, wenn der mittlere Stundenverbrauch 12 ½ Gallons (oder Liter) ist?

14 / 15

Beispiel 10

Bekannt: Die verbrauchte Quantität (Gallons oder Liter), die Zeit.
Unbekannt: Stundenverbrauch.
Nach einer Flugdauer von 145 Minuten (2 Stunden 25 Min.) stellt der Pilot fest, dass er 27 ½ Gallons (oder Liter) Benzin verbraucht hat. Welches ist der mittlere Stundenverbrauch?

LÖSUNG: Die Ziffer 12½ der weissen Skala wird dem Stundenmerkzeichen gegenübergestellt. Das Resultat wird auf der äusseren schwarzen Skala abgelesen gegenüber der Ziffer 60 der weissen Skala: 288 (oder 4 Stunden 48 Minuten auf der inneren schwarzen Skala).

LÖSUNG: Die Ziffer 27½ (oder 27,5) der weissen Skala wird der Ziffer 145 der äusseren schwarzen Skala gegenüber gestellt. Das Resultat wird auf der weissen Skala abgelesen gegenüber dem Stundenmerkzeichen: 11,3 Gallons (oder Liter) in der Stunde.

DURCH-SCHNITTLICHER HÖHENGEWINN (oder Höhenverlust)

Zwei der nachstehenden Grössen sind bekannt, um diese Probleme zu lösen: Höhe, Zeitdauer, mittlerer Höhengewinn oder -verlust.

Beispiel 11

Bekannt: Zeitdauer, durchschnittlicher Höhenverlust.

Unbekannt: Höhe.
Ein Flugzeug verliert durchschnittlich 300 Fuss (oder Meter) Höhe in der Minute. Welches ist sein totaler Höhenverlust nach 34 Min.?

LÖSUNG: Die Ziffer 30 (= 300) der weissen Skala wird dem Einheitsmerkzeichen (10 auf der äusseren schwarzen Skala) gegenüber gestellt. Das Resultat wird auf der weissen Skala abgelesen gegenüber der Ziffer 34 der äusseren Skala: 10'200 Fuss (oder Meter).

Beispiel 12

Bekannt: Zeitdauer, Höhe.
Unbekannt: Durchschnittlicher Höhengewinn.
Ein Flugzeug gewinnt 6900 Fuss (oder Meter) in 15 Minuten. Welches ist sein durchschnittlicher Höhengewinn?

16 / 17

LÖSUNG: Die Ziffer 6900 der weissen Skala wird der Ziffer 15 der äusseren schwarzen Skala gegenüber gestellt. Das Resultat wird auf der schwarzen Skala abgelesen gegenüber dem Einheitsmerkzeichen: durchschnittlicher Höhengewinn 460 Fuss (oder Meter) in der Minute.

Beispiel 13

Bekannt: Durchschnittlicher Höhengewinn, Höhe.
Unbekannt: Zeitdauer.
Ein Pilot steigt um 7400 Fuss (oder Meter) mit einem durchschnittlichen Höhengewinn von 500 Fuss (oder Meter) in der Minute. Wieviel Zeit hat er benötigt?

LÖSUNG: Die Ziffer 500 der weissen Skala wird dem Einheitsmerkzeichen (10 auf der äusseren schwarzen Skala) gegenüber gestellt. Das Resultat ist auf der weissen Skala abzulesen gegenüber der Ziffer 7400 der weissen Skala 14,8 Minuten.

DISTANZ BEIM AUFSTEIGEN UND LANDEN

Zwei der nachstehenden Grössen sind bekannt: Distanz, Zeitdauer, Geschwindigkeit. Die Anwendung des Navitimers ist die gleiche wie in den Beispielen 4, 5 und 6.

Beispiel 14

Der Pilot im Beispiel 13 will die Distanz kennen, die sein Flugzeug zurückgelegt hat, wenn sein Aufstieg beendet ist. Die durchschnittliche Geschwindigkeit ist 120 Meilen (oder km) mit einem Rückenwind von 20 Stundenmeilen (oder Std./km).

LÖSUNG: Die Ziffer 140 (120+20) der weissen Skala wird dem Stundenmerkzeichen MPH gegenüber gestellt. Das Resultat wird auf der weissen Skala abgelesen gegenüber der Ziffer 14,8 (siehe Resultat Beispiel 13) und ist: 34,5 Meilen (oder km).

18 / 19

UMWANDLUNG VON SEEMEILEN, STATUARISCHEN MEILEN ODER KILOMETERN

Auf der äusseren schwarzen Skala findet man die Angaben: NAUT. (= Seemeilen), STAT. (= Statuärische Meilen) KM. (= km). Die Umwandlung von stat. Meilen in Seemeilen oder in km (oder

umgekehrt) kann ohne weiteres auf der weissen Skala abgelesen werden.

Beispiel 15

Bekannt: 60 stat. Meilen.
Unbekannt: Seemeilen.

LÖSUNG: Die Ziffer 60 der weissen Skala wird der Benennung STAT. der äusseren schwarzen Skala gegenüber gestellt. Das Resultat wird auf der weissen Skala abgelesen gegenüber der Benennung NAUT.: 52 Seemeilen.

Beispiel 16

Bekannt: 60 stat. Meilen.
Unbekannt: km.

LÖSUNG: Die Ziffer 60 der weissen Skala wird der Benennung STAT. der äusseren schwarzen Skala gegenüber gestellt. Das Resultat wird auf der weissen Skala abgelesen gegenüber der Benennung KM.: 96,5 km.

20 / 21

BREITLING
IM WUNDERLAND

Lösen Sie
Ihre komplizierten Probleme
mathematisch,
einfach,
rasch mit dem

CHRONOMAT
Chronograph + Rechenscheibe

BREITLING
GENÈVE

INHALTSVERZEICHNIS

ALLGEM. BESCHREIBUNG

DES BREITLING-CHRONOMAT

Das Zifferblatt des Breitling-Chronomat unterscheidet sich von dem eines gewöhnlichen Chronographen durch das Fehlen des Tachymeters, Telemeters und des Pulsometers. Diese letzteren sind durch zwei Skalen ersetzt : die eine am äusseren Rand des Zifferblattes, die andere auf der drehbaren Lünette. Passend angewendet, erlauben diese Einteilungen alle mathematischen Operationen, aufgebaut : a) auf der mittels des chronographischen Zeigers registrierten Zeit, b) auf allen kaufmännischen und technischen Problemen. Ausserdem ist der Breitling-Chronomat, wie jeder übliche Chronograph, mit den chronographischen Einteilungen von Sekunde und 1/5 Sekunde versehen.

2 · 3

DAS ABLESEN DER SKALEN

Die innere Skala (auf dem Zifferblatt) wird von links nach rechts gelesen, während die äussere Skala (auf der drehbaren Lünette) von rechts nach links gelesen wird. Das Ablesen dieser Skalen geschieht auf die gleiche Art und Weise, wie das Ablesen eines Thermometers. Die kleinen Striche zwischen zwei Ziffern (z. B. zwischen 5 und 6) stellen den Wert von 1/10 dar, d. h. 5,1 - 5,2 - 5,3 usw.

SCHÄTZUNG DER ZIFFERN

Auf den Skalen sind einzig die Einheiten dargestellt, so dass alle Dezimalen in Gedanken aufgehoben werden müssen. Dagegen wird das Komma (od. evtl. Nullen) beim Ablesen des Resultates wieder hinzugefügt. Die Praxis wird jede Unsicherheit in dieser Hinsicht beseitigen.

BEISPIEL : Die Ziffer 32 angewendet als Marschkontrolle = 3,2 km. Std., angewendet beim Radrennen = 32 km. Std., angewendet als Fluggeschwindigkeit = 320 km. Std.

TACHYMETER

Zweck : Feststellung der Geschwindigkeit eines Läufers, eines Fahrzeuges, eines Flugzeuges, einer Bewegung usw. Der Breitling-Chronomat gestattet die Ausführung aller tachymetrischen Berechnungen und zwar auf einer beliebigen Streckenlänge, und während einer beliebigen Zeitdauer.

GEBRAUCHSANWEISUNG

Man findet auf der inneren Skala 4 rote Merkzeichen :
1/5 (auf der Zahl 18, denn 18 000 1/5-Sekunden = 1 Stunde) ; S (auf der Zahl 36, denn 3600 Sekunden = 1 Stunde) ; Minutes (auf der Zahl 6, denn 60 Minuten = 1 Stunde) ; H (auf der Zahl 1). 1 Stunde ist Basiseinheit für alle Berechnungen.

HAUPTREGEL

Die Länge der kontrollierten Strecke ist immer dem entsprechenden Merkzeichen, das als Rechnungsgrundlage dient, gegenüber zu stellen :

1/5	wenn das chronometr. Resultat in 1/5 Sek. ist				
S	»	»	»	in Sek.	»
Minutes	»	»	»	in Min.	»
H	»	»	»	in Std.	»

4 · 5

Die Beobachtungszeit erhält man durch das Ingangsetzen und Anhalten des grossen Stoppzeigers mittels des oberen Drückers. Diese Zeit wird umgewandelt in 1/5 Sekunden, in Minuten oder Stunden, je nach dem Merkzeichen, das für die in Frage kommende Berechnung gewählt und angewendet wird.

BEISPIELE: PROBLEM ❶

Ein Kraftwagen durchfährt 1 km in 40 Sekunden. Welches ist seine Geschwindigkeit ? (in km Std.)

LÖSUNG : 1 (Streckenlänge) auf der äusseren Skala, wird dem Merkzeichen S (Zeitmass) gegenübergestellt. 4 (40 Sekunden Fahrtdauer) deckt sich mit 9. Resultat : 90 km Std.

PROBLEM ❷

Ein Skispringer macht einen Sprung von 55 Meter Länge und braucht dazu 3 2/5 Sekunden. Welches war die Stundengeschwindigkeit dieses Sprunges ?

LÖSUNG : 55 (Sprunglänge) wird auf den Merkpunkt 1/5 eingestellt. (1/5 = Zeitmass) 3 2/5 Sekunden = 17 Fünftel. 17 und 58 fallen zusammen und ergeben ein Resultat von : 58 km Std.

PROBLEM ❸

Ein Läufer verwendet 19 Minuten für eine Strecke von 3,5 km. Welches ist die Stundengeschwindigkeit ?

LÖSUNG : 35 (3,5 km) gegenüber dem Merkzeichen « Minutes » (chronometrierte Zeit). 19 (Dauer des Laufes) deckt sich mit 11, d. h. Stundengeschwindigkeit dieses Laufes : 11 km.

6 · 7

PROBLEM ❹

Ein Geher durchläuft 52 km in 15 Std. Welches ist seine Stundengeschwindigkeit ?

LÖSUNG : 52 (52 km) gegenüber dem Merkzeichen H (Zeitnehmung in Stunden). 15 (Marschdauer) fällt mit 34,6 zusammen (,6 schätzungsweise). Stundengeschwindigkeit : 3 km 460 m. Dieses Beispiel ist charakteristisch, was die Plazierung des Kommas anbetrifft.

EIN WICHTIGER VORTEIL

DES BREITLING-CHRONOMAT

Wohnt man einem Rennen bei, so stellt man ein für alle Mal die Zahl ein, die die Länge der Rennstrecke darstellt, und zwar gegenüber dem Merkzeichen, das für die chronometrischen Beobachtungen gewählt wurde. (Sekunde, Minute usw.) Die Skala gibt nun nach jeder Runde die Stundengeschwindigkeit der Konkurrenten an.

BEISPIEL: PROBLEM ❺

Länge der Piste : 6 km 330 m. (Runde in 2 Min. 40 Sek., (d. h. 160 Sek.) = 140 km Std.

Dieses Beispiel ist auf dem Merkzeichen S aufgebaut (S = Sekunden).

8 · 9

126

Der Breitling-Chronomat erlaubt auch die

SCHÄTZUNG
DER STRECKENLÄNGE

selbst wenn nur die Geschwindigkeit bekannt ist, mit der diese Strecke durcheilt wurde. Es genügt, die vorstehenden Beispiele umzukehren.

PROBLEM ❻

Beispiel Nr. 1 in umgekehrtem Sinn. Ein Automobil fährt während 40 Sekunden mit einer Stundengeschwindigkeit von 90 km. Welches ist die durchfahrene Distanz?

LÖSUNG: 90 (Geschwindigkeit) wird 40 (Kontrolldauer) gegenübergestellt. Abgelesen beim Merkpunkt S (Zeitmass) ergibt das Resultat von 1, = befahrene Strecke 1 km.

10

Verwandlung von

Km-Stunden in
Meter-Minuten
Meter-Sekunden

In gewissen Fällen (in der Armee, beim Brieftaubendienst usw.), können solche Verwandlungen nützlich sein.

PROBLEM ❼

Verwandlung von 54 km-Std. in Meter-Minuten und Meter-Sekunden.

LÖSUNG: 54 gegenüber H (Stunden). Lese beim Merkzeichen « Minutes »: 9, d. h. 900 Meter-Minuten, und beim Merkzeichen S: 15, d. h. 15 Meter-Sekunden.

11

RADSPORT

Gebrauch des Breitling-Chronomat als Geschwindigkeitsmesser für Radfahrer.

GEBRAUCHSANWEISUNG

Folgende Rechnungsgrundlagen sind unentbehrlich:
1. Grösse der verschiedenen Uebersetzungen; 2. 10 Pedaldrehungen.

 BEISPIEL · PROBLEM ❾

Ein Radfahrer fährt mit einer Uebersetzung von 4,5 m. Welches ist seine Stundengeschwindigkeit?

LÖSUNG: 4,5 (Grösse der Uebersetzung) wird gegenüber dem Merkzeichen S (Sekunden) gesetzt. Wenn nun für 10 Pedaldrehungen 16 Sekunden gebraucht wurden, ergibt sich bei der Zahl 16 das Resultat und zwar: 1 = eine Stundengeschwindigkeit von 10 km.
BEMERKUNG: Es ist darauf zu achten, dass beim Ingangsetzen des Chronographen bei der ersten Pedaldrehung in Gedanken mit Null zu zählen begonnen wird und nicht mit 1.

12

TELEMETER

ZWECK: Feststellung der Distanz zwischen zwei durch Licht und Ton verbundene Punkte. (Einschlagspunkt eines Blitzes, Geschützstellung oder Stellung eines Schiffes usw.).

GEBRAUCHSANWEISUNG

Durch Gegenüberstellung des Merkzeichens «Telemeter» (rot auf der äusseren Skala) und der die chronometrierte Zeit darstellenden Zahl, liest man beim Merkzeichen 0 (Sekunde, wenn das registrierte Resultat in Sekunden ist) die vom Ton durcheilte Distanz.

BEISPIEL · PROBLEM ⓿

Ein Donnerschlag wird 4 Sekunden nach der Wahrnehmung des Blitzes vernommen. In welcher Distanz hat der Blitz eingeschlagen?

LÖSUNG: Merkpunkt «Telemeter» gegenüber 4 (4 Sekunden). Beim Punkt S wird abgelesen: 13,3 (,3 schätzungsweise). Durcheilte Distanz = 1 km 330 m.

13

PULSOMETER

Schnelle Berechnung der Zahl der Pulsschläge eines Kranken in der Minute.

GEBRAUCHSANWEISUNG

Gegenüber dem Merkzeichen « Minutes », (gewünschtes Resultat in Min.) wird die Anzahl der gezählten Pulsschläge gestellt. Die Anzahl der Pulsschläge pro Minute kann bei der Sekundenzahl, die die Beobachtungszeit darstellt, abgelesen werden.

BEISPIEL: PROBLEM ❿
Ein Arzt zählt 27 Pulsschläge in 24 Sekunden. Wieviel sind es in der Minute?

LÖSUNG: 27 (Pulsschläge) gegenüber dem Merkzeichen « Minutes ». Ablesen der Zahl bei 24 (Beobachtungsdauer). Resultat: 67 Pulsschläge in der Minute.
WICHTIGE BEMERKUNG: Man achte darauf, dass beim Ingangsetzen des Stoppers nicht mit der Zahl 1 begonnen wird, denn der Abgang des Stoppzeigers ist gleichwertig mit 0.

14

TAKTZÄHLER

Taktkontrolle:

GEBRAUCHSANWEISUNG

Gleiches Verfahren wie beim Pulsometer.

BEISPIEL: PROBLEM ⓫

8 Takte sind in 7 Sekunden ausgeführt worden. Wieviele Takte sind es in der Minute?

LÖSUNG: 8 (Anzahl der Takte) gegenüber dem Merkzeichen « Minutes ». Bei der Zahl 7 (Beobachtungsdauer) steht das Resultat, nämlich 68 Takte in der Minute.
WICHTIGE BEMERKUNG: Man achte darauf, dass beim Ingangsetzen des Stoppers nicht mit der Zahl 1 begonnen wird, denn der Abgang des Stoppzeigers ist gleichwertig mit 0.

15

PRODUKTIONSZÄHLER

Berechnung der Produktion pro Minute, Stunde usw.

GEBRAUCHSANWEISUNG

Wenn die Zeitnehmung in Sekunden geschah, ist die Zahl 1 der äusseren Skala vis-à-vis von «S» einzusetzen; im Falle der Messung in Minuten, vis-à-vis von « Minutes ». Die stündliche Produktion wird gegenüber der Ziffer abgelesen, welche die Anzahl der während der Kontrolldauer fabrizierten Stücke darstellt.

 BEISPIEL: PROBLEM ⓬

In 4 Sekunden fabriziert eine Maschine 1 Stück. Welches ist die stündliche Produktion?

LÖSUNG: Zahl 1 beim Merkzeichen S. Gegenüber 4 erscheint das Resultat, d. h. 900 Stück in der Stunde.

16

METEOROLOGIE

Je nach der Höhe einer Wolke kann auf der nephoskopischen Egge die Strecke gemessen werden, die von der Wolke zwischen 2 Zähnen zurückgelegt wurde. Die geschätzte Höhe einer Wolke ist 10mal grösser als die visierte Strecke. Folglich wird die Zahl 5 auf das Merkzeichen S (Sekunden) eingestellt, wenn die angenommene Höhe der Wolke 5000 m und die Beobachtungsdauer 24 Sekunden ist. Ihre Geschwindigkeit beträgt also 75 km Std., denn 24 deckt sich mit 75.

17

STUNDENZÄHLER

Ist eine Zeitdauer von mehreren Stunden zu chronometrieren, so genügt es, das Merkzeichen « 1 » der drehbaren Lünette gegenüber dem Stundenzeiger einzustellen. Auf diese Weise wird der Zeitpunkt des Beobachtungsbeginns festgehalten.

18

HANDEL UND TECHNIK
DIE MULTIPLIKATION

Der Multiplikand wird dem Multiplikator gegenübergestellt, d. h. vis-à-vis von « 1 » der einen oder anderen Skala kann das Resultat abgelesen werden.

BEISPIEL: PROBLEM ⓭

$3 \times 18 = 54$

19

DIVISION

Die Division geht in umgekehrter Weise vor sich, indem die Zahl « 1 » der einen oder anderen Skala dem Dividenden gegenübergestellt wird, was eine ganze Reihe Divisionen hervorbringt, die Resultate gegenüber dem Divisor abgelesen werden können, d. h. jeder gewählte Divisor deckt sich mit dem Resultat.

 BEISPIEL: PROBLEM ⓮

$54 : 18 = 3$
$54 : 45 = 1,2$

20

DREISATZ

Aus den vorstehenden 2 Regeln geht hervor, dass auf dem Breitling-Chronomat die Multiplikation und die darauf folgende Division in einer einzigen Operation ausgeführt werden können.

BEISPIELE: PROBLEM ⓯

$$\frac{3 \times 18}{12} = 4,5$$

21

Wenn 1,5 m ...... (1)
Fr. 9.— kosten ..... (2)
kosten 6 m .... (3)
X .... (4)

PROBLEM 16

PROZENTRECHNUNG

BEISPIEL: PROBLEM 17

LÖSUNG : (2) und (3), d. h. Fr. 9.— und 6 m einander gegenüberstellen und das Resultat des Problems (4) bei (1), d. h. 1,5 m ablesen. Resultat : 6 Meter kosten Fr. 36.—.

Die Schwierigkeit besteht darin, dass das Problem richtig gestellt wird. Man bemerkt z. B., dass die Nummer (1) und (3) (Meter) einander gleichen. Ebenso verhält es sich mit den Zahlen (2) und (4) (Franken), d. h. die Zahlen (1) und (4) sind gegensätzlich. Wenn also die Meter gegeben sind, wird ein Resultat in Franken gesucht. Auch die mittleren Nummern (2) und (3) sind von verschiedener Natur.

Die Berechnung der Prozente ist ein gebräuchlicher Dreisatz und das Verfahren ist das gleiche wie oben, d. h. 85 % von 48 = X. In der Tat, wenn 100 % zu 85 % werden, dann wird 48 zu X. Es genügt, die einfache Multiplikation von 85 × 48 auszuführen, um das Resultat bei « 1 » auf der einen oder anderen Skala ablesen zu können, d. h. 41.

22   23   24

EINSTANDSPREIS-BERECHNUNGEN

BEISPIELE: PROBLEM 18

I. Ein Kaufmann wünscht auf dem Verkaufspreis eines Artikels 30 % zu gewinnen. Folglich muss er ihn zu Fr. 100.— verkaufen, wenn er Fr. 70.— dafür bezahlt hat. Welches ist der Verkaufspreis eines Artikels, der ihn Fr. 6.— kostet ?

LÖSUNG : Gegenüberstellung von « 1 » und Ankaufspreis. Bei der Zahl 70 befindet sich das Resultat : Fr. 8.60, weniger 30 % = Fr. 6.—.

II. Ein Kaufmann wünscht auf dem Ankaufseines Artikels 30 % zu gewinnen. Folglich muss Fr. 130.— verkaufen, was ihn Fr. 100.— kostet, der Ankaufspreis wird mit 130 vervielfacht. (100 Ankaufspreis + 30 % Gewinn auf demselben.)

PROBLEM 19

Ein Artikel kostet Fr. 6.—, zu wieviel muss er verkauft werden, wenn man 30 % gewinnen will ?

LÖSUNG : Gegenüberstellung von 6 und 13 (F und Ablesen des Resultates bei « 1 » auf eine Skalen : = Fr. 7.80.

III. Ein schwierigeres Problem :

PROBLEM 20

Ankauf einer Ware à Fr. 6.— das kg brutto. Verpackungsverlust ist 10 %. Welches ist der Preis von 1 kg netto ?

LÖSUNG : Gegenüberstellung von 6 (Franken) und « 1 » einer Skala und Ablesen des Resultates bei 9 (900 g), ergibt : Fr. 6.70 das kg netto.

BERECHNUNG DES TRIEBSTOFFVERBRAUCHS

eines Automobils in %

BEISPIEL: PROBLEM 21

Ein Auto verbraucht auf 130 km 23 Liter Benzin. Wieviel verbraucht es für 100 km ?

LÖSUNG : Die Anzahl der Liter wird bei « 1 » auf eine der Skalen eingestellt und das Resultat bei der Zahl, die die durcheilten km darstellt, abgelesen, d. h. 18 Liter Verbrauch für 100 km.

26   27   28

ZINSRECHNUNGEN

Erinnern Sie sich der Zinsnummern und der Zinsdivisoren ? Wenn man « 1 » beim Merkzeichen S plaziert (360 Tage = 1 kaufmännisches Jahr), erhält man eine Tabelle dieser Zinsdivisoren und zwar :

4 % = Zinsdivisor	**90**
5 % = »	**72**
6 % = »	**60**

Man multipliziert das Kapital mit der Anzahl der Tage, dividiert durch den Zinsdivisoren und erhält das Resultat gegenüber dem Zinsdivisor. (Prinzip des Dreisatzes.)

BEISPIEL: PROBLEM 22

Wieviel Zins bringt ein Kapital von Fr. 400.— während 180 Tagen à 4 % ?

LÖSUNG : Gegenüberstellung von 4 (400.—) und 18 (180 Tage). Ablesen des Resultates bei 9 (90 = Zinsdivisor von 4 %) d. h. Fr. 8.—.

KURSUMRECHNUNGEN

Durch das Gegenüberstellen der Zahlen « 1 » Skalen erhält man eine Tabelle, die die Kursur nungen gestattet.

BEISPIEL: PROBLEM 23

Arg. Pesos 100.— sind in Zürich zu SFr. 5.— notiert. Wieviel arg. Pesos erhält man für 100 Schweizer Franken ?

LÖSUNG : Man stellt die Ziffern « 1 » der Skalen einander gegenüber und liest das Resultat (Kurs der arg. Pesos) = 2000, d. h. SFr. 100.— einen Wert in arg. Pesos 2000.—.

GEOMETRISCHE RECHNUNGEN

BEISPIELE: PROBLEM 24

Welches ist der Umfang eines Kreises vom Durchmesser 7 m ?

LÖSUNG : Formel ⌀ × π.
Die Ziffer « 7 » der äusseren Skala auf π der Innenskala einstellen und das Resultat auf der Innenskala bei « 1 » (rotes H) ablesen, nämlich 21,98 oder 22m.

PROBLEM 25

Wie gross ist die Fläche des Kreises von Problem No. 24?

LÖSUNG : Formel π × r².
Um r zu bestimmen, wird der Durchmesser durch 2 dividiert — eine Operation, die im Kopf durchgeführt wird : 7 : 2 = 3,5. Nun wird der Wert « 3,5 » der äusseren Skala auf 3,5 der Innenskala gedreht und das Resultat der Multiplikation bei « 1 » (rotes H) abgelesen, nämlich 12,25.
Dann dreht man « 12,25 » der Aussenskala auf π der inneren Skala und das Endresultat der Rechnung wird bei « 1 » (rotes H) abgelesen, nämlich : 38,46 oder 38,5 m².

a)   b)

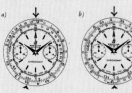

Chronographs of the forties, all in 18-karat gold. Top row: $4500-5000 ea.; Center row: left to right $2500-3000, $4200-4500; Bottom row: $4500-5000 ea.

Chrono-"Callisto" (left). $1200-1500

Chrono-"Sextant" (right), $1200-1500

Breitling "J-Class" (left). $1200-1500

Breitling "J-Class" (right), $850-950

"Navitimer" in gold, circa 1967 (left). $5000-5500

"Cosmonaute" in gold, circa 1967 (right). $6000-7000

"Navitimer" in platinum, limited edition (left). $4500-5000

"Cosmonaute" presently in production (right). $10,000-11,000

"Old Navitimer", new version. $3000-3500

"Chronomat", circa 1942. $2000-2200

"Navitimer" with the old "AOPA" lettering in the emblem, circa 1952. $1800-2000

"Reserve de Marche" (with up and down indicator), presently in production. $4000-4500

Breitling "Shark" (left). $1800-2000

Breitling "Professional" (right). $1200-1400

Breitling "Duograph" (left). $5000-5500

"New Pluton" (right). $1100-1200

"UTC", the world's smallest quartz watch, integrated into the band (left). $3000-3500

"Chrono "Longitude" (right). $4500-5000

Breitling "Professional" (left). $2200-2400

"Astromat", Chrono "QP", the top-line product by Breitling, with perpetual calendar (right). $33,000-34,000

"Nightflight" for ladies (above). $1500-1800

"Nightflight". $1500-1800

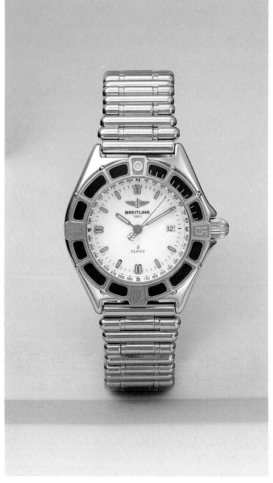

"J-Class" (below). $2200-2400

Advertisement for the Cosmonaute that went into space in 1962.

Watch in Space!

**This watch orbited the earth
in May 1962.
It is the Navitimer, the watch
that timed the Astronauts,
produced by**

Breitling

**Geneva
Appointed Watchmaker
to World Aviation**

Breitling Watch Corp. of USA

15 West 47th St. New York 36 (N.Y.)

"Navitimer QP", 1993. $25,000-30,000

BREITLING
1884

BREITLING AND THE PROBLEM OF FAKES

BREITLING has long been a renowned brand name, and is therefore an easy target for product pirating of all kinds.

In protecting its rights, BREITLING places the highest value on its unique creations and manufacturing processes, which have international model and patent protection. This applies to the highly developed functions, the designs and the outstanding finish of their watches. The following examples show what inimitable achievements are embodied in every BREITLING watch.

◀ The CHRONO-COCKPIT has more than 450 parts, which are assembled in more than a hundred expert work processes. The finished piece is usually tested thoroughly under extreme conditions. Only after this can the name of quality go on.

▲ The dial of the COSMO-NAUTE is produced according to a very special technique passed down from olden times: black paint is applied to a silver surface, whereby the smallest surface detail is preserved. The tritium numerals can also be read without difficulty in the dark. The preparation of such a dial demands at least forty work processes.

▶ At BREITLING the scratchproof sapphire glass is made non-reflecting: the process removes optical disturbances and protects the dial from dangerous UV rays. Also, legibility is heightened and the beautiful appearance of the watch is brought to its full splendor.

▲ The case of a BREITLING watch, on account of its particular structure, requires extremely complex work processes, which make falsification difficult.

For example, every scale on the dial and every step on the lunette of this SIRIUS model must be cut individually by means of laser technology, which makes it impossible to forge.

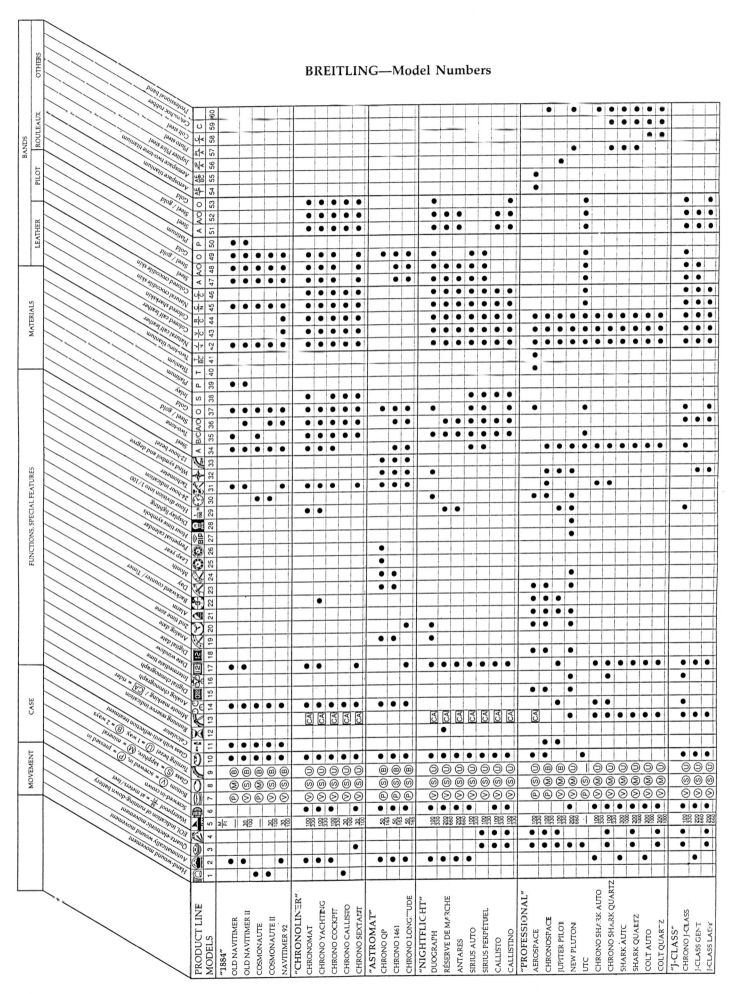

"Navitimer Rattrapante", 1993-94. $22,000-24,000

View from the rear

Views of the movement. Left, the rotor of solid 18-karat gold; right, Caliber 34 chronograph movement with sweep hand

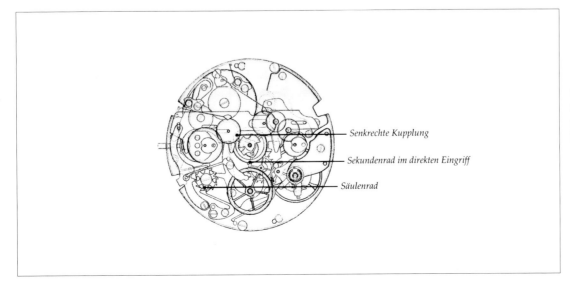

— Senkrechte Kupplung

— Sekundenrad im direkten Eingriff

— Säulenrad

Drawing of the Caliber 34 movement, diameter 25.60 mm = 11.5 lignes, 6.90 mm high, 39 jewels

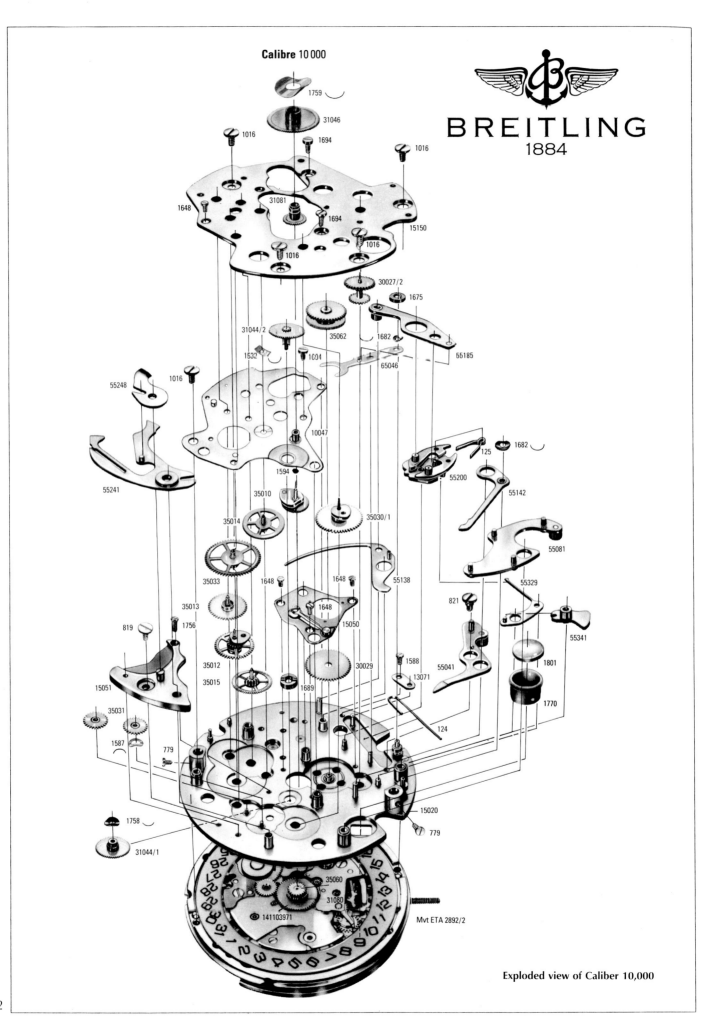

Calibre 10 000

BREITLING
1884

Exploded view of Caliber 10,000

142

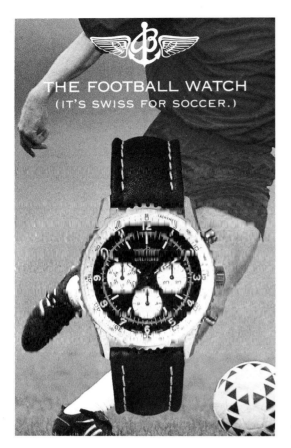

THE FOOTBALL WATCH
(IT'S SWISS FOR SOCCER.)

Breitling advertisement at the time of the 1994 World Soccer Championship in the USA, "The Football Watch", offered only as a limited edition. $12,000-14,000

*Der erste Serien-*CHRONOMAT, *speziell für die Frecce Tricolori entwickelt.*

Page from the Breitling brochure "10 Years of Chronomat", showing cockpit. $2200-2500

"Navitimer Airborne", 1993. $3000-3500

"Navitimer AVI", 1993. $2500-2800.

"Old Navitimer QP", 1993. $4500-4800

"Chronomat Longitude", 1993. $2800-3000

"Chronomat", 1994, decorative edition set with diamonds. $24,000-26,000

"Callistino Automatic", 1993. $1200-1500

"Sirius Lady Perpetual", 1994. $1200-1500

"Antares World", 1993. $1500-1800

"Navitimer 1461", 1993.
$24,000-26,000

Chrono "Shark Yacht-ing", 1993. $2800-3000

"Chronomat", 1994. $2800-3000

Chrono "Colt", 1993.
$2500-2700

Chrono "Sirius", 1993. $3000-3200

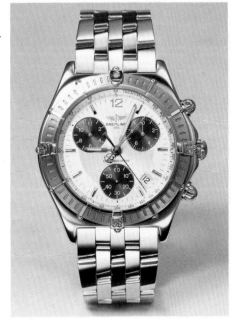

Flight Watches

Flight watches are those used on board aircraft. Because of the way and where they are used, they are more exposed to external influences, yet must perform their service as precision instruments under these environmental conditions. This requires special engineering measures, beginning in the design phase. Also, these watches undergo special regulatory specifications, similar to chronometers, the strictest of which are the so-called military specifications. The watches are tested on a shaking table, must come through several hundred complete operations of the control buttons, and their accuracy is tested at various temperatures, whereby the case is placed in various positions for certain lengths of time. The hands are treated with luminous material, so that good legibility in darkness is guaranteed. Most of these watches have a start-stop mechanism, in order to measure flight times on a certain heading or other time measurements needed to calculate such things as fuel consumption.

The mechanical on-board watches are, as a rule, fit with 6- or 8-day movements.

Various on-board watches, produced between 1936 and 1950. Top left: $200-300; Top right: $200-300; Bottom center: $300-350.

Top: $200-300; Center: $300-400; Bottom: $300-350.

Top row: $300-400 ea.; Center row: $400-450 ea.; Bottom center: $1500-1800.

Reference Numbers

Why are there reference or serial numbers? What significance do they have, and what are they used for?

These are the kinds of questions that arise when we speak of the reference numbers on the watch cases. The situation is rather like that of the caliber numbers used by the raw-movement manufacturers, who stamp a number into the movement. When replacement parts are needed in any way, one can refer to these numbers and obtain parts even after years have passed because they are matched precisely to the given movement.

It is just the same with the finished watches, which have a corresponding number on the case bottom as a number for all replacement parts, including hands, dials and crowns. This number can reveal, in coded form, the year of manufacture or other important information for the watch manufacturer. For example, the reference number 806 S was given to the Navitimer, and specifically the hand-wound version in steel with the Venus movement, production of which began at Breitling in the fifties. Since these reference num-

bers are also closely linked with the serial numbers in production records, it is possible to determine the exact date of manufacture for any watch. Thus one sees how important the reference number is, and that the two reference numbers, namely that of the raw-movement manufacturer and that of the watch manufacturer, do not necessarily have to have anything to do with each other. In addition, Breitling also signs the case with the typical "B", and the firm's name is also found on the balance mount. This use of the reference number to identify a watch was formerly not done with such precision, and only since the thirties has a meaningful system been hidden behind the numbers. The series numbers were formerly not maintained in a definite form either, so that the dating of very old Breitling watches is not very simple.

Today it is all the simpler, since Breitling itself uses a different reference number for every modification to any basic model.

Markings on the case lids of Breitling watches include the series number (large number) and the reference number (small number).

List of Reference Numbers

This list of reference numbers includes the reference numbers of most of the watches produced by Breitling, with short notes about their specialties. This list will make possible identifying a Breitling watch as such and place it in a definite series. The numbers are listed in numerical order within a certain cat egory, such as men's wristwatches, chronographs, etc. But this does not necessarily mean that the watches were all produced in the same year. Nor does the list make any claim to completion. In conjunction with the caliber list, one can also determine which movement should be housed in which watch

Ref.No.	Name	Description	Stopwatches
25	Montbrillant	min.-1/5 sec.	
32	Montbrillant	Tachometer scale, 30 min.	
34		16", 30 min.	
40		30 min.,/sweep hand	
42		Pulsation scale, basis 30	
44		Tachometer scale, basis 1000 m	
47		Tachometer scale, basis 200/1000 m	
48		Pocket watch with chronograph, 30 min., production scale	
49		Pocket watch with chronograph, 30 min./10 revolution scale	
50	Montbrillant	Pocket watch with chronograph, 45 min./decimal scale	
51	Sprint	Pocket watch with chronograph, 45 min./soccer timer	
52		Pocket watch with chronograph, 1/10 sec.--15 min.	
56		Pocket watch with chronograph, extra-flat version	
57		Pocket watch with chronograph, tachometer scale, ectra-flat version	
501		1/5 sec.--30 min., one button	
502		1/5 sec.--20 min.	
502/10		1/10 sec.--15 min.	
502/9	Yachting Timer	5 min.	
502/16	Football Timer	45 min.	
502/18		1/5--1/10--30 min., separate stop button	
502		Like 1501 but with Rosskopf movement	
502/18		Like 1518 but with Rosskopf movement	
502/10		Like 1505 but with Rosskopf movement	
502/18/10		Like 1518/10 but with Rosskopf movement	
502/9		Like 1509 but with Rosskopf movement	
503		1/5 sec.,--30 min,. flat glass type	
504		1/5 sec.--30 min., no kuevette	
505		1/10 sec.--15 min.	
506		1/10 sec.--15 min., flat glass	
507		1/10 sec.--30 min.	
508		1/5 sec.--60 min.	
509	Yachting	5 min. counter	
510		Tachometer scale, basis 1000 m	
511		Tachometer scale, basis 100, 200,300 m (police)	
512		Tachometer scale, quarter-mile/hour	
513		Stopwatch with production dial	
514		Pulsometer scale, basis 15	

Ref No	Name	Description
515		1/100 min.(Breitling monogram on dial)
515		1/10 sec.
516	Football	45 min.
517	Football	45 min., anti-zero setting lock
518		1/5 sec., extra zero-setting button
518/10		1/10 sec., extra zero-setting button
519		1/16 sec.
520		1/20 sec.--5 min.
521		1/30 sec.--5 min.
522		1/50 sec.
523		1/100 sec.
524		1/100 sec.--3 min. 20"
524NR		1/100 sec.--3 min. 22" black dial
525		1/100 sec., 1 revolution/sec.
526	Radium	1/5 sec.--30 min.
527		1/10 sec.--15 min.
528		1/5 sec., permanent running
530		1/5 sec.--30 min. 28"
531	Yachting Timer	1 sec.--5 min., 28"
532	Compass Uhr	Radiocounter to find a ship's location
533	Compass Uhr	1/5 sec. permanent running
533/17	Compass Uhr	1/5 sec. permanent running
533		1/100 sec.--60 min., 28"
534	Compass Uhr	1/10 sec.--15 min.
535		1/100 min., 1 revolution in 100 sec.
537	AWF 2	1/5 sec. with stopping at any time
538		1/5 sec.--60 min.--12 hrs.
539		1/50 sec.--3 min.
540		1/100 sec.--30 min.
541		1/5 sec., extra-strong case
542		1/30 sec.--10 min.
543		1/1000 hr., 1 revolution in 36 sec.
545	Ruder Stoppuhr	
546	Water Polo	Polo timing
547	Ice Hockey	Hockey timing
549	Boxing Timer	
550	AWF 1	1/5 sec.--60 min.
551		1/5 sec., permanent running with stop
554		1/5 sec.--30 min., decimals
555		Waterproof, 1/5 sec.--30 min.
556		1/5 sec.--30 min., ink-dot stopper
558		1/100 sec.,permanent running with stop
560		1/10 sec., permanent running with stop
561		1/10 sec.--30 min. 28"
562		AWF 31/100 sec.--60 min.--12 hrs.
563	Präzisionsstoppuhr	1/50 sec.--3 min.
564	Präzisionsstoppuhr	1/100 sec.--3 min.
565		Combination with minute counter, 19"
566		1/5 sec., central hr. & min. counter
567		1/5 sec.
568		1/10 sec., double dial
569		1/10 sec.
570		1/50 sec.--3 min., fine chronograph
571		1/100 sec.--3 min., fine chronograph
572	Militär. Tachymeter	1/30 sec./basis 50 m
573	Militär. Tachymeter	1/60 sec./basis 300 m
612 GF		Precision chronograph, double hands,1/10 sec. in big stopwatch case

Ref.No.	Name	Description
1501		30 min. counter, start-stop via crown
1505		30 min. counter, start-stop via crown
1506		Like 1505 but with 30 min. counter
1508		Like 1501 but with 60 min. counter
1509		5 min. counter for sport sailing
1509/8		Like 1509 but with 10 min. counter
1511		1/5 sec., 30 min. counter, with 4 separate scales to measure speed
1518		1/5 sec., 30 min. counter
1518/8		Like 1518 but with 60 min. counter
1518/10		1/10 sec., with 15 min. counter
1518/10/6		Like 1518/10 but with 30 min. counter
1524		1/100 sec., 3 min. counter, one-hand stopper
1528		1/5 sec., 30 min. counter, one-hand stopper
1528/10		Like 1528 but with 1/10 sec. & 15 min. counter
1528/RI		Like 1528 with 1/5 sec., side zero-setting
1528/10/RI		Like 1528 with 1/10 sec., side zero setting
1533	Doppelzeiger-Stoppuhr	30 min.
1534	Doppelzeiger-Stoppuhr	15 min.
1538		1/5 sec., 60 min & 12-hr. counters
1542		1/10 sec., 5 min, counter, 1 rev. of central second in 10 sec.
1542/8		Like 1542 but with 10 min. counter
1575	Tel-Rad	1/5 sec., 60 min. counter, one-hand stopper, for use in filming
1576		1/5 sec., 60 min. counter, for ice hockey and soccer
2533		Split second stopwatch, 1/5 sec., 30 min. counter
2534		Like 2533 with 1/10 sec. & 15 min. counter
2540		Like 2533 with 1/100 sec., one rev. of central second in 3 sec., 3 min. counter
3533		Like 2533 with 11-jewel movement
3534		Like 2534 with 11-jewel movement
3537		1/5 sec., 30 min. counter, double hand
3569		Like 3537 with 1/10 sec.

Ref.No.	Name	Description	Men's Wristwatches
TO-2	Trans-Ocean	Round gold case, central second, date	
TO-1	Trans-Ocean	Round steel case, central second, date	
1/260	Unitime	Round case, central second, date, world time zones, automatic	
45/1		Round gold case, automatic	
51/26	Automatic	Round case, central second, date, automatic	
54/26	Unidate	Round case, central second, date, automatic	
55/26	Unidate	Round case, central second, date, automatic	
57/26	Unidate	Square case, central second, date, automatic	
58/26	Unidate	Round case, central second, date, automatic	
59/26	Unidate	Round case, central second, date, automatic	
60/26	Unidate	Round case, central second, date, automatic	
62/26	Unidate	Round case, central second, date, automatic	
66		Round case, central second, date, automatic	
66		Round case, central second, date, automatic	
84/28		Round case, central second, full calendar, moon phase, automatic	
86/28		Round case, central second, full calendar, moon phase, automatic	
88/28		Round case, central second, fullcalendar, moon phase	
89/28	Datora	Round case, central second, full calendar, moon phase, automatic	
90/28	Datora	Autom.Round case, central second, full calendar, moon phase	
93/28		Round case, central second, full calendar, moon phase	
94/28		Round case, central second, full calendar, moon phase	
140/20		Round case, small second, date, calendar	

Ref.No.	Name	Description
140/20		Round case, small second, full calendar
199/19		Round case, small second
224/25		Round case, central second, automatic
236/25		Round case, central second, automatic
236/25	Automatic	Round case. central second, automatic
238/25		Round case, central second, automatic
239/95		Round case, central second, full calendarwith moon phase
244/94		Round case, central second, full calendarwith moon phase
807 A	Super Ocean	Round case, central second, automatic
925/21	Automatic	Square case, central second, automatic
1059/29		Round case, central second
1060/29		Round case, central second
1097/22		Round case, central second
1098/22		Round case, central second
1099/22		Round case, central second
1100/22		Round case, central second
1207/19		Round case, small second
1211/19		Round case, central second, double ring of numerals
1212/19		Round case, small second
1213/19		Round case
1214/19		Round case, small second
1215/19		Round case, small second, recessed crown
1216/19JC		Round case, playing-card design on dial
1216/19SC		Round case, picture of saint on dial
1216/19WB		Round case, coat of arms on dial
1216/19G		Round case, small second
1216/19N		Round case, small second
1217/19		Round case, small second, recessed crown
1352		Round 18-K gold case, small second
1354		Round case, small second, strong band attachments
1355		Round case, central second
1356		Round case, small second, gold-plated
1911		Round 18-K gold case
2400/24		Round case, central second
2401/24		Round case, central second, recessed crown
2402/24		Round case, central second
2501/25		Round case, central second, automatic
2501/25	Automatic	Round case, central second, automatic
2502/25	Automatic	Round case, central second, automatic
2503/25		Round case, central second, automatic
2504/25		Round case, central second, automatic
2505/25		Round case, central second, automatic
2506/25		Round case, central second, automatic
2507/25		Round case, central second, automatic
2508/25	Chronomat	Round case, central second, turningbezel for calculating
2509/25	Automatic	Round case, central second, automatic
2509		Round case, central second, automatic, waterproof
2514		Round 18-K case, central second, black dial, automatic
2515		Round steel case, central second
2515		Round case, central second, automatic
2516		Round case, central second, gold-plated
2516		Round case, central second
2516		Round case, central second, automatic, waterproof
2517		Round case, central second, automatic, waterproof, outside band attachments
2518		Round steel case, central second
2518		Round case, central second
2518		Round case, central second, automatic, waterproof, slightly recessed crown

Ref.No.	Name	Description
2519		Round case, central second, automatic, waterproof
2520		Round gold case, central second, automatic
2520		Round 18-K case, central second, automatic, waterproof
2521		Round gold case, central second, automatic
2521		Round case, central second
2521		Round case, central second, automatic, waterproof, outside band attachments
2522		Round gold case, central second, date, automatic
2523		Round case, central second
2524		Round case, wide rim, central second
2525		Round case, central second, slightly rounded band attachments
2526		Round case, central second, semi-recessed crown
2527		Round case, central second, very archedglass
2528		Round case, central second
2529		Round case, central second
2530		Round case, central second
2531		Round case, central second, very small band attachments
2532		Round case, central second
2601		Round case, central second, date,automatic, waterproof
2602		Round case, central second, automatic, waterproof, date, outside band attachments
2603		Round case, central second, automatic, waterproof, date
2604		Round steel case, central second, date
2605		Round gold case, central second, date, automatic
2605		Round 18-K case, central second, date, waterproof, automatic
2606		Round gold case, central second, date, automatic
2606		Round 18-K case, central second, date, waterproof, automatic, outside attachments
2607		Round 18-K case, central second, date
2608		Round 18-K case, central second, date
2609		Round case, central second, date, diagonal band attachments
2610	Unitime	Round case, central second, date, turninglunette for world time
2611		Round case, central second, date
2612		Round case, gold inlay, central second,date
2612		Round case, central second, date, blackrim
2613		Round case, central second, date, very arched glass
2614		Round case, central second, date
2615		Round case, central second, date
2616		Round case, central second, date
2617		Round case, central second, date
2900/29		Round case, central second
2905/29		Round case, central second
2906/29		Round case, central second
2907		Round case, central second, wide rim,waterproof
2917		Round case, central second, gold-plated
2917		Round case, central second, very flat, waterproof
2924	Derby	Round case, central second
2924	Sport	Round case, central second
2926		Round case, central second, wide rim
2927		Round 18-K case, central second
2928		Round case, central second, waterproof
2929		Round case, central second, waterproof
2930		Round gold case, central second, ultra-flat
2930		Round case, central second
2930		Round 18-K case, central second
3931		Round case, central second, sturdy bandattachments
2932		Round case, central second, gold-plated, rounded band attachments
2933		Round case, central second

Ref No	Name	Description
2934		Round case, central second, very archedglass, very thin rim
2935		Round case, central second, semi-recessedcrown
2936		Round case, central second, gold-plated
3301		Round case, central second, gold-plated
3302		Round 18-K case, central second, waterproof
3306		Round 18-K case, central second
3307		Round case, central second, gold-plated
4001		Round case, central second, date,waterproof
4002		Round case, central second, date, gold-plated, waterproof
4003		Round case, central second, date, wide rim
4004		Round case, central second, date
4005		Round case, central second, date
4006		Round case, central second, date
4007		Round gold case, central second, date, automatic
4008		Round case, central second, date
4009		Round case, central second, date, gold-plated
4010		Round 18-K case, central second, date, very arched glass
4501		Round case, small second
4506		Round 18-K case, small second, extra flat
4510		Square gold case
4511		Round 18-K case, extra flat
4512 S		Square steel case
4512 P		Square case, gold-plated
4513		Round steel case, extra flat
4514		Round gold case, extra flat
4515		Round case
4516		Round case, gold-plated
4517		Round case, gold-plated
4519		Round case
6003		Square gold case, fixed band
7102		Round case, central second, square dial
7105/19		Round 18-K case, central second
7107/19		Round case, small second
7110		Round gold case, central second, ultra-flat
7110		Round case, central second
7110		Round case, small second
7111		Round case, central second
7112		Round case, central second
7113		Round case, central second
7114		Round case, central second
7119		Round case, small second, black dial
7120		Round case, small second
7122		Round case, central second
7123		Round case, central second
7131		Round gold case, central second
7146/20		Square 18-K case, small second,calendar
7150		Round case, small second
7151		Round case, small second
7153		Round case, central second, date
7156		Round case, central second
7171		Round case, small second
7172		Round case, small second
7175		Round gold case, small second
7176		Round gold case, small second
7177		Round gold case, small second
7178		Round gold case, small second
7179		Round gold case, small second
7182		Square gold case, small second

Ref.No.	Name	Description
7183		Square gold case, small second
7190		Round gold case, small second
7193		Round gold case
7195		Round gold case, small second
7197		Square gold case, small second
7801		Square case, small second
7802/84		Square 18-K case, wide rim
7809		Round case, central second
7010		Square case, central second
71753		Round case, small second, date

Ref.No.	Name	Description	
			Ladies'
			Wristwatches
TO-7	Trans-Ocean	Round gold case	
TO-6	Trans-Ocean	Round case, gold-plated	
TO-5	Trans-Ocean	Round steel case	
932		Round case, central second, large diameter	
2000-52		Round case	
2002/52		Round case, leather band	
2003/52		Square case	
2007/52		Square case, wide rim	
2008/52		Round case	
2201/85		Round case, central second	
3200/71		Round case, central second	
5017/50		Round case	
5037		Square 18-K case	
5200/2		Square case	
5201/2		Square case	
5202/2		Round case	
5205/2		Square case, wide rim	
5206/2		Square case	
5215		Round case, fixed band attachments	
5216		Round case	
5217		Round case	
5218		Round case, dark rim	
5219		Round case	
5506		Square 18-K case	
5506		Round case, fabric band	
5509		Round white-gold case	
5518		Square case, gold-plated, oversize	
5520		Round case, gold-plated	
5531		Round case	
5536		Oval case, wide rim, crown at 12	
5537		Oval case, crown at 12	
5538		Pointed oval case, small version	
5539		Oval case, wide rim	
5545		Square case, attachments at corners, crown on the side by the 4	
5547		Square case, band attachments off center	
5549		Round case, wide rim, band attachments off center	
5550		Triangular case, crown by the 9	
5591		Round case, gold-plated	
5592		Round case, gold-plated	
5593		Round case, gold-plated	
5594		Round case, gold-plated	
5595		Square case, gold-plated	
5596		Round 18-K case	

Ref.No.	Name	Description
5597		Round 18-K case
5598		Round 18-K case
5599		Round 18-K case
5600		Round 18-K case, pointed attachments
5601		Round 18-K case
5602		Round 18-K case
5603		Round 18-K case, offset attachments
5604		Round 18-K case
5605		Round 18-K case
5607		Square 18-K case, wide rim
5616		Round white-gold case with diamonds
5617		Round white-gold case with diamonds
5624		Round gold case
5624		Round 18-K case
5626		Round 18-K case
5628		Round case
5629		Round case, gold-plated
5630		Round case, gold-plated
5631		Round case, gold-plated
5632		Round case, gold-plated, wide rim
5633		Round case
5634		Round case, wide band attachments
5635		Round 18-K case
5637		Round 18-K case
5638		Square 18-K case
5639		Oval 18-K case
5640		Oval 18-K case, wide rim
5641		Round 18-K case, stylish attachments
5642		Round 18-K case
5643		Square 18-K case, wide rim
5644		Square 18-K case, very wide rim
5645		Square 18-K case
5647		Round gold case
5649		Square gold case
6052		Round gold case, fixed band
6053		Round gold case
6060		Round case, sturdy band attachments
6750		Round steel case
6751		Round case, gold-plated
6752		Round gold case
6753		Round case, cut glass
6754		Round gold case
6756		Round case
6757		Round case
6758		Round gold case
6759		Round gold case
6760		Round case, perforated band attachments
6761		Round case
6762		Round case, stylish band attachments
6763		Round case
6764		Round case, gold-plated
6764		Round case, gold-plated
6769		Square gold case, wide rim
7105		Round case, gold-plated, second hand
7106		Round 18-K case, second hand
7107		Round case, gold plated
7108		Round 18-K case
7110		Round gold case, central second

Ref.No.	Name	Description
7151		Square gold case, cloth band
7500		Square case, chain band on case
7502		Square case, cloth band
7506		Square case, leather band
7511		Square case, leather band
7512		Square case, leather band
7519/50		Square 18-K case, band attachments on long sides
7529		Square gold case, leather band
7533		Square gold case, cloth band
7534		Square gold case, dark dial, leather band
7540/50		Square 18-K case, wide attachments
7561		Square gold case, cloth band
7562		Square gold case, cloth band
7563		Square case, leather band
7564		Square gold case, leather band
7566		Square gold case, cloth band
7570		Square gold case, chain band fixed to case
7571		Square gold case, cloth band
7572		Round gold case, cloth band
7573		Square gold case, cloth band
7574		Square gold case, cloth band
7576/50		Square 18-K band, ball-shaped corners
7598/51		Square 18-K case
7599/51		Square 18-K case
7600/51		Square 18-K case
7701		Round case, leather band
7702		Round case, leather cord band
7710		Round case
7720		Round gold case, cloth band
8503		Round 18-K case, small second
8505		Round 18-K case
8506		Round 18-K case
9201		Round case

Ref.No.	Name	Description	Chronographs
170		Hand-wound, round case, square buttons,45-minute counter	
171		Hand-wound, round case, square buttons,45-minute counter, Roman numerals	
172		Hand-wound, round case, square buttons,telemetric scale	
173		Hand-wound, round case, square buttons,pulsation scale	
174		Hand-wound, round case, square buttons,tachometer scale	
175		Hand-wound, round case, round buttons, wide rim with turning lunette, 12-hour division	
176		Hand-wound, round case, square buttons,tachometer scale	
178		Hand-wound, round case, square buttons	
179		Hand-wound, round case, square buttons,hours marked with lignes	
612		Hand-wound, stopwatch case, sweep hand	
701		Hand-wound, round case, square buttons,large numbers	
701/2		Hand-wound, round case, square buttons,30-minute counter, various scales	
709		Hand-wound, round case, square buttons,45-minute counter, various scales	
710 E		Hand-wound, round case, square buttons, 30-minute counter, tachometer scale	
710 B		Like 710 E but with telemetric scale	
711 E		Hand-wound, round case, square buttons,small second	
711 M		Like 711 E but with pulsation scale	
711 B		Like 711 E but with telemetric scale	
711 AU		Hand-wound, round case, wide rim, blackluminous dial, round buttons, military version	

Ref.No.	Name	Description
711 AG		Hand-wound, round clip case, small second, square buttons, telemetric scale
711	Reinc	Hand wound, round clip case, small second, square buttons, pulsation scale
716		Hand-wound, round case, square buttons, 30 minute counter, projecting attachments
717		Hand-wound, round case, square buttons, 30 minute counter, flexible attachments
718 O.K.		Hand-wound, round clip case, squarebuttons, various scales
718		Hand wound, round case, square buttons, 30 minute counter, various scales, worn on a chain
720		Hand-wound, round case, square buttons, 30 minute counter
721		Hand-wound, round case, square buttons, 30 minute counter, projecting attachments
722		Hand-wound, round case, rectangularbuttons, 30 minute counter
723		Hand-wound, round case, square buttons, 30 minute counter, massive attachments
724		Hand-wound, round case, square buttons, 30 minute counter, telemetric counter,stylish band attachments
725		Hand-wound, round case, square buttons, 30 minute counter, black dial, flowingattachments
726		Hand-wound, round case, square buttons, 30 minute counter, very large attachments
727		Hand-wound, round case, square buttons, 30 minute counter
728		Hand-wound, round case, square buttons,various scales
729		Hand-wound, round case, square buttons, 30 minute counter, wide attachments
732		Hand-wound, round case, square buttons, 30 minute counter, curved attachments
733		Hand-wound, round case, square buttons, 30 minute counter, projecting attachments
734		Hand-wound, round case, square buttons, 30 minute & 12 hour counters
734		Round case, square buttons, 30 minute & 12 hour counters, tachometer scale
753		Hand-wound, round case and buttons, 30 minute counter
754		Hand-wound, square case & buttons, 30minute counter
755		Hand-wound, square case & buttons, noscales
756		Hand-wound, square case & buttons, 30minute counter, various scales
757		Hand-wound, square case and buttons
760		Round case, square buttons, 45 minute counter
762		Duograph Hand-wound, round case, square buttons, 45 minute counter
764		Duograph Hand-wound, round case & buttons, 45 minute counter
765	Premier	Hand-wound, round case & buttons, 30 minute & 12 hour counters
765 AVI		Hand-wound, round case & buttons, blackdial, 15 minute & 12 hour counters
766	Duograph	Hand-wound, round case, square buttons, 30 minute & 12 hour counters, dual crown use
767		Hand-wound, round case & buttons, luminous black dial, military version
769	Chronomat	Hand-wound, round case, square buttons, 45 minute counter, turning bezel calculator
769	Chronomat	Round case, square buttons, turninglunette calculator
770		Hand-wound, round case, square buttons, 45 minute counter
771		Hand-wound, round case, square buttons, 45 minute counter
772		Hand-wound, round case, square buttons, 45 minute counter, black dial
773		Hand-wound, round case, square buttons, 45 minute counter, tachometer scale
775		Hand-wound, round case, square buttons, 45 minute counter, tacho- & telemeter scales
777		Round case & buttons, 45 minute counter
778		Hand-wound, round case, square buttons, 45 minute counter, sturdy band attachments

Ref.No.	Name	Description
779		Hand-wound, round case, square buttons, 45 minute counter
780		Hand-wound, round case, square buttons, 45 minute counter
781		Hand-wound, round case, square buttons, 45 minute counter, black dial
782		Hand-wound, round case, square buttons, 45 minute counter, various scales
783	Duograph	Hand-wound, round case, square buttons, 45 minute counter, dual crown function
784	Duograph	Hand wound, round case, square buttons, 30 minute counter, calendar
785	Datora	Round case, square buttons, 30 minute & 12 hour counters, date, calendar
786	Chronomat	Hand-wound, round case, square buttons, 30 minute & 12 hour counters, turning bezel calculator
787	Premier	Hand-wound, round case, square buttons, 30 minute & 12 hour counters
788	Premier	Hand-wound, round case & buttons, 30 minute & 12 hour counters
789		Round case, square buttons, 45 minute counter
790		Hand-wound, round case & buttons, 45 minute counter
791	Duograph	Hand-wound, round case & buttons, 30 minute & 12 hour counters
792		Hand-wound, round case, square buttons, big numerals, 45 minute counter
793		Hand-wound, round case, square buttons, 45 minute counter, Roman numerals
794		Hand-wound, round case, square buttons, 45 minute counter, sturdy band attachments
795		Hand-wound, round case, square buttons, 45 minute counter, curved band attachments
796		Hand-wound, round case, square buttons, 45 minute counter
798		Hand-wound, round case, square buttons, 45 minute counter
799		Hand-wound, round case, square buttons, 30 minute & 12 hour counters, small date ring
800		Hand-wound, round case, square buttons, 30 minute & 12 hour counters, date, moon phase, duograph function
801	Chronomat	Hand-wound, round case, square buttons, 30 minute & 12 hour counters, date, moon phase, turning bezel calculator
803	Datora	Round case & buttons, 30 minute & 12 hour counters, date, calendar
804	Datora	Hand-wound, round case & buttons, 30 minute & 12 hour counters, full calendar with moon phase
805	Datora	Hand-wound, round case, square buttons, 30 minute & 12 hour counters, full calendar with moon phase
805	Datora	Round case, square buttons, 30 minute counter, full calendar with moon phase
806/3	Navitimer	Hand-wound, small steel case
806/4	Navitimer	Hand-wound, small gold-plated case
806/5	Navitimer	Hand-wound, small 18-K gold case
806/5	Navitimer	Hand-wound, small gold case, date
808/3	Chrono-Matic	Hand-wound, small steel case
808/4	Chrono-Matic	Hand-wound, small gold-plated case
808/5	Chrono-Matic	Hand-wound, small gold case
809/3	Cosmonaute	Hand-wound, small steel case
809/4	Cosmonaute	Hand-wound, small gold-plated case
809/5	Cosmonaute	Hand-wound, small 18-K gold case
812	GMT	Hand-wound, large steel case
814 N	Top Time	Hand-wound, square case, dark dial
814 YN	Top Time	Hand-wound, square case, light dial
815/3	Long Playing	Hand-wound, round case, light dial
815/4	Long Playing	Hand-wound, round gold-plated case, light dial
816	Navitimer	Hand-wound, large steel case
818	Chrono-Matic	Hand-wound, large steel case
819	Cosmonaute	Hand-wound, large steel case
820/3	Long Playing	Hand-wound, oval case, black dial
820/4	Long Playing	Hand-wound, oval gold-plated case, gold dial
1151		Hand-wound, round case, square buttons, 45 minute counter
1180		Round case, square buttons, 30 minute counter
1188		Hand-wound, round case, square buttons, 45 minute counter
1189		Hand-wound, round case, square buttons, heavy numerals

Ref.No.	Name	Description
1190		Round case, square buttons, 30 minute counter
1191		Round case & buttons, 30 minute counter
1192		Round case, square buttons, 30 minute counter
1193		Round case, square buttons, 30 minute counter
1194		Hand-wound, round case, square buttons, 45 minute counter
1197	Cadette	Hand-wound, round case, square buttons, 45 minute counter
1198		Hand-wound, round case, square buttons, 45 minute counter
1199		Hand-wound, round case, square buttons, 45 minute counter
1577	Chronoslide	Stopwatch with turning bezel & calculator
1765	Unitime	Hand-wound, steel case, 24-hour dial
1806	Navitimer	Automatic, large steel case, date
1806-M	Navitimer	Automatic, small matte-black case, date
1808	Chrono-Matic	Automatic, large steel case, date
1809	Cosmonaute	Automatic, large steel case, date
2005	Super Ocean	Hand-wound, round case & buttons, turning bezel, diver's watch
2010 N	Sprint	Hand-wound, round case, dark dial
2010 CR	Sprint	Hand-wound, round case, divided dial
2016 or	Sprint	Hand-wound, fixed bezel, 45-minute counter
2016 gr	Sprint	Like 2016 or but with green dial
2016 br	Sprint	Like 2016 or but with brown dial
2016 bl	Sprint	Like 2016 or but with blue dial
2018/1	Datora	Like 2016 or, oval case, date
2018/4	Datora	Hand-wound, oval gold-plated case, date
2030 D	Datora	Hand-wound, square case, black dial, date
2030 YN	Datora	Hand-wound, square case, white dial, date
2031 N	Datora	Hand-wound, round case, black dial, date
2031 ST	Datora	Hand-wound, round case, white dial, date
2033	Datora	Hand-wound, semicircular case, date
2034/T	Datora	Hand-wound, oval case, tachometer scale, white dial
2034	Datora	Tachometer scale, dark dial
2100		Round case, square buttons, 30 minute counter
2105	Chrono-Matic	Automatic, large round case, round buttons, turning bezel, date, Super Ocean
2110-B	Chrono-Matic	Automatic, small case, white dial, date
2110-N	Chrono-Matic	Automatic, small case, black dial, date
2111-B	Chrono-Matic	Like 2122-N but with white dial
2111-N	Chrono-Matic	Automatic, square case, black dial, date
2111-ST	Chrono-Matic	Automatic, square case, white dial, date
2112-HB	Chrono-Matic	Automatic, oval case, white dial, date
2112-MN	Chrono-Matic	Automatic, oval case, black dial, date
2114 N	Chrono-Matic	Automatic, oval steel case, black dial
2114 T	Chrono-Matic	Automatic, oval case, tachometer scale
2114 P	Chrono-Matic	Automatic, oval case, pulsometer scale
2114 D	Chrono-Matic	Automatic, oval case, decimal scale
2115	GMT	Automatic, large steel case, date
2117 bl	Pult	Automatic, 30 minute & 12 hour counters, blue dial, date
2117 br	Pult	Like 2117 bl but with brown dial
2118-B	Chrono-Matic	Automatic, square gold case, date
2118-N	Chrono-Matic	Automatic, square case, dark blue dial, date
2119/B	Trans-Ocean	Automatic, oval case, white dial, date
2119/C	Trans-Ocean	Automatic, oval case, blue dial, date
2120-B	Chrono-Matic	Automatic, round case & buttons, 30 minute counter, date, crown by the 9
2120-N	Chrono-Matic	Like 2120-B but with black dial
2121	Chrono-Matic	Automatic, square case, round buttons, 30 minute counter, date, crown by the 9
2122-N	Chrono-Matic	Automatic, oval case, round buttons, 30 minute counter, date, black dial, crown by the 9
2205	Super Ocean	Steel, large second hand turns once per hour
2211 YN	Top Time	Hand-wound, square case, light dial

Ref.No.	Name	Description
2211 D	Top Time	Hand-wound, square case, dark dial
2212 N	Sprint	Hand-wound, oval case, dark dial
2214 ST	Sprint	Hand-wound, oval case, light dial
3100-A	Pluton	Quartz, analog & digital time, turning bezel with compass design
3100-M	Pluton	Like 3100-A but with 12-hour bezel lignes
3300-A	Jupiter	Quartz, analog & digital time, turning bezel for various calculations
3300-BC	Jupiter	Like 3300-A but two-tone
3300-GP	Jupiter	Like 3300-A but gold-plated
3865		Automatic steel diver's watch for men, date
3962		Like 3865 but lady's model
7101 br	Pult	Chronograph, hand-wound, tablet case, brown dial, date, 30 minute & 12 hour counters, turning bezel
7101 bl	Pult	Like 7101 br but with blue dial
7102/A	Pult	Hand-wound, oval case, brown & white dial, date
7102/B	Pult	Like 7102/A but with blue & white dial
7102/C	Pult	Like 7102/A but with all-blue dial
7103	Long Playing	Hand-wound, semicircular case, dark dial, date
7104	Long Playing	Hand-wound, oval case, dark dial, date
7104 T	Long Playing	Hand-wound, oval case, light dial, date
7650	Co Pilot	Hand-wound, small steel case
7651	Co Pilot	Automatic, large steel case, date
7652	Co Pilot	Hand-wound, large steel case
7661	Yachting	Automatic, large case, date
7662	Yachting	Automatic, large case, date, hand-wound
7806	Navitimer	Hand-wound, small steel case, date
810.3 N	Top Time	Hand-wound, round case, dark dial
810.3 YN	Top Time	Hand-wound, round case, light dial
810.4 N	Top Time	Hand-wound, round gold-plated case, dark dial
810.4 YN	Top Time	Hand-wound, round gold-plated case, light dial
824.3 N	Top Time	Hand-wound, round case, dark case, 24 hours
824.4 N	Top Time	Hand-wound, round gold-plated case, dark dial, 24 hours
8806	Navitimer	Automatic, small steel case
8806/5	Navitimer	Automatic, small gold case
9106	Navitimer	Large steel case, LED shown, 15 functions
2004.5 B	Top Time	Hand-wound, round gold case
2004.5 N	Top Time	Hand-wound, round gold case, dark dial
2004.5 YN	Top Time	Hand-wound, round gold case
2007.1 B	Top Time	Hand-wound, square polished case, light dial
2007.1 YN	Top Time	Hand-wound, square steel case, dark auxiliary dial
2007.1 CR	Top Time	Hand-wound, square steel case
2007.1 BR	Top Time	Hand-wound, square steel case, dark dial
2009.4 B	Top Time	Hand-wound, square polished gold case, light dial
2009.4 YN	Top Time	Hand-wound, square gold-plated case, dark auxiliary dial
2009.4 CR	Top Time	Hand-wound, square gold-plated case
2009.4 B	Top Time	Hand-wound, square gold-plated case, dark dial, tachometer & pulsometer scales, orange dial
80191	Pluton	Quartz chrono with analog & digital time
80520-1	Callisto	Hand-wound, sapphire glass, dark dial, 30 minute & 12 hour counters
80520-2	Callisto	Like 80520-1 but with gold auxiliary dials
80520-3	Callisto	Like 80520-1 but with white dial
80520-4	Callisto	Like 80520-1 but with silver auxiliary dials
80520-5	Callisto	Like 80520-1 but with white auxiliary dials
80900	Maritim	Hand-wound, wide turning bezel with 60-minute markings, date
80975	Jupiter	Quartz chrono, analog time, date, 12-hour counter
81600-1	Navitimer	Hand-wound, new version of Navitimer Old
81600-2	Navitimer	Like 81600-1 but gold-plated
81600-3	Navitimer	Like 81600-1 but solid gold
81600-3	Cosmonaute	New version of Cosmonaute Old

Ref.No.	Name	Description
81600-4	Cosmonaute	Like 81600-3 but gold-plated
81600-5	Cosmonaute	Like 81600-3 but solid gold
81610	Navitimer	New automatic version of Navitimer Old
81950-1	Chronomat	Automatic, black dial, date, 30 minute & 12 hour counters
81950-2	Chronomat	Like 81950-1 but with white dial
81950-3	Chronomat	Like 81950-1 but with gold auxiliary dials
81950-4	Chronomat	Like 81950-1 but with white dial
81950-11	Chronomat	Like 81950-1 but with an added quartz watch integral with the band

Breitling Since 1980

Ref.No.	Name	Description	Ref.No.	Name	Description
B 10047/48	Antares	Bicolored	B 15507	Duograph	Bicolored
D 10047/48	Antares	18-K gold	K 15507	Duograph	18-K gold case
K 10067	J-Class Gent	18-K gold	A 17035	Colt	Automatic, steel case
D 10067	J-Class Gent	Steel/gold case	A 17605	Shark	Automatic
A 10071	Sirius	Automatic, steel case	J 18405	Astromat QP	Yellow gold case
B 10071	Sirius	Automatic, bicolored	K 18405	Astromat QP	18-K gold case
D 10071	Sirius	Automatic, steel/gold case	A 19022	Navitimer QP	Steel case, perpetual calendar, no leap year
K 10071	Sirius	Automatic, 18-K gold	A 19405	Astromat	Steel case
			D 19405	Astromat	Steel/gold case
A 10096	Colt Military	Steel military watch	J 19405	Astromat	Yellow gold case
B 11045/46	Callisto	Bicolored	K 19405	Astromat	18-K gold case
D 11045/46	Callisto	Steel/gold case	A 20048	Chronomat Longitude	Automatic, steel case, second time
K 11045/46	Callisto	18-K gold case	A 20405	Longitude	Steel case
A 12019	Cosmonaute	Steel case	D 20405	Longitude	Steel/gold case
B 12019	Cosmonaute	Bicolored	J 20405	Longitude	18-K yellow gold case
K 12019	Cosmonaute	18-K gold case	K 20405	Longitude	18-K gold case
A 12020	Cosmonaute 2	Steel case	H 29020	Navitimer QP	Rose gold case, perpetual calendar
B 12020	Cosmonaute 2	Steel/gold case			
D 12020	Cosmonaute	Steel/gold bezel, hand-wound	J 29020	Navitimer QP	White gold case, perpetual calendar
K 12020	Cosmonaute 2	18-K gold case	L 29020	Navitimer QP	Platinum case, perpetual calendar
A 13019	Old-Navitimer	Steel case			
B 13019	Old-Navitimer	Bicolored	A 30011	Cockpit	Steel case
K 13019	Old-Navitimer	18-K gold case	B 30011	Cockpit	Bicolored
L 13019	Old-Navitimer	Platinum case	D 30011	Cockpit	Steel/gold case
A 13020	Old Navitimer 2	Steel case	K 30011	Cockpit	18-K gold case
D 13020	Old Navitimer 2	Steel/gold case	A 30012	Chrono Cockpit	Automatic, steel case
K 13020	Old Navitimer 2	18-K gold case	B 30012	Chrono Cockpit	Automatic, steel/gold rider
L 13020	Old Navitimer 2	Platinum case			
A 13023	Navitimer AVI	Steel case, automatic	D 30012	Chrono Cockpit	Automatic, steel/gold lunette
A 13047/48	Chronomat	Steel case			
B 13047/48	Chronomat	Bicolored	K 30012	Chrono Cockpit	Automatic, 18-K gold
C 13047/48	Chronomat	Steel/gold case	A 30021	Navitimer 92	Steel case
D 13047/48	Chronomat	Steel/gold case	D 30021	Navitimer 92	Steel/gold case
H 13047/48	Chronomat	18-K rose gold case	K 30021	Navitimer 92	18-K gold case
K 13047/48	Chronomat	18-K gold case	A 30022	Navitimer 92	Automatic, steel case
A 13048	Chronomat Yachting	Automatic, steel case	D 30022	Navitimer 92	Automatic, steel/gold bezel
B 13048	Chronomat Yachting	Automatic, steel/gold case			
J 13048	Chronomat	18-K yellow gold case	K 30022	Navitimer 92	Automatic, 18-K gold
			A 33030	Navitimer Airborne	Automatic, steel case
A 13051	Shark	Automatic chronograph	D 33030	Navitimer Airborne	Automatic, steel/gold bezel
B 14047	Reserve de Marche	Bicolored	K 33030	Navitimer Airborne	Automatic, 18-K gold case
D 14047	Reserve de Marche	Steel/gold case	A 50035	Colt	Quartz, steel case
K 14047	Reserve de Marche	18-K gold case	M 50035	Colt	Black case
B 14948	Res. de Mar./Antares	Bicolored	A 51037	New Pluton	Steel case

Ref.No.	Name	Description	Ref.No.	Name	Description
B 52043/44	Callistino	Bicolored	A 57035	Colt	Quartz, steel case
B 52043/44	Callistino	Steel/gold case	B 57045	Callisto	Bicolored case
K 52043/44	Callistino	18-K gold case	D 57045	Callisto	Steel/gold case
B 52045	Callistino II	Quartz, steel/gold rider	A 58605	Shark	Quartz
D 52045	Callistino II	Quartz, steel/gold bezel	A 59027/28	Jupiter Pilot	Steel case
K 52045	Callistino II	Quartz, 18-K gold case	A 60141	UTC	Steel case, 22 mm
D 52063	J-Class Lady	Steel/gold case	B 60141	UTC	Bicolored, 22 mm
K 52063	J-Class Lady	10-K gold case	K 60141	UTC	10-K gold, 22 mm
D 52065	J-Class Lady II	Quartz, steel/gold bezel	A 61072	UTC	Steel case, 20 mm
K 52065	J-Class Lady II	Quartz, 18-K gold case	B 61072	UTC	Bicolored, 20 mm
A 53011	Chrono Sirius	Quartz, steel case	E 61072	UTC	Titanium case, 20 mm
B 53011	Chrono Sirius	Quartz, steel/gold rider	K 61072	UTC	18-K gold case, 20 m
A 53067	J-Class Chrono	Steel case	F 61072	UTC	Bicolored titanium case, 20 mm
D 53067	J-Class Chrono	Steel/gold case			
K 53067	J-Class Chrono	18-K gold case	A 62011	Sirius	Quartz, steel case
A 53065	Shark	Quartz chronograph	B 62011	Sirius	Quartz, bicolored case
B 55045	Sextant	Bicolored	D 62011	Sirius	Quartz, steel/gold case
D 55045	Sextant	Steel/gold case	K 62011	Sirius	Quartz, 18-K gold case
K 55045	Sextant	18-K gold case	B 62021	Sirius Lady	Quartz, steel/gold rider
A 56011	Chronospace	Steel case			
E 56059	Aerospace	Titanium case	D 62021	Sirius Lady	Quartz, steel/gold bezel
F 56059	Aerospace	Bicolored			
J 56059	Aerospace	18-K gold case	K 62021	Sirius Lady	Quartz, 18-K gold case

Ref.No.	Name	Description	
617		Chronograph for aircraft	**On-Board Watches**
618-12-10		To military specifications MIL-C-9196, 8-day movement, 12 hours, 2nd time zone via chrono	
618-12-24-10		Like 618-12 but with 12- & 24-hour indication	
618-24-10		Like 618-12 but with 24-hour indication	
619		Two 12-hour indications with separate hands	
620		Like 619 but with single 12-hour indication	
118-12-24-10 ET		8-day movement with separate 12- and 24-hour indications	
118-12-24 W		To military specifications SM-C 349904, 539475, 8-day movement with separate 12- and 24-hour indication	
640-12-10		To military specifications MIL-C 9196, 8-day movement, 12-hour indication plus chrono-part with minute and 12-hour indications	
640-24-10		Like 540-12 but with 24-hour indication	
643		8-day movement with 24-hour indication plus chrono-part with minute and 12-hour indications	
645		Modified to military specifications, 8-day movement, 24-hour indication with second time zone	
633		Like 618 but in a different case	
634		Like 618 but in a much smaller case	
636		On-board watch with large second and small 12-hour indication	

Calibers Used

Ref.No.	Caliber	Ref.No.	Caliber	Ref.No.	Caliber
1/260	Felsa260	816	Venus 178	2112	Breitling 12
22/29	FEF 350	817	Valjoux 236	2114	Breitling 11
34	Valjoux 7731	818	Venus 178	2118	Breitling 12
42	FHF 186	819	Venus 178	2119	Breitling 12
170	Venus 170	820	Valjoux 7736	2205	Venus 188
171	Venus 188	824	Venus 178	2212	Valjoux 7733
178	Venus 170	828	Venus 178	2214	Venus 178
180	Venus 170	932	Felsa 700	2522	Felsa 4000
605-A	Valjoux 5	1155	Valjoux 7730	2523	Felsa 4000
734	Venus 178	1156	Valjoux 7730	2524	Felsa 4000
760	Venus 176	1158	Valjoux 7730	2525	Felsa 4000
762	Venus 179	1159	Valjoux 7730	2526	Felsa 4000
765	Venus 178	1185	Venus 188	2527	Felsa 4000
766	Venus 178	1188	Venus 188	2528	Felsa 4000
769	Venus 170	1189	Venus 188	2529	Felsa 4000
769	Venus 176	1190	Venus 188	2530	Felsa 4000
777	Venus 176	1191	Valjoux 7733	2531	Felsa 4000
778	Venus 152	1191	Venus 188	2608	Felsa 4002
779	Venus 176	1192	Venus 188	2609	Felsa 4002
780	Venus 176	1193	Venus 188	2611	Felsa 4002
781	Venus 176	1194	Venus 188	2612	Felsa 4004
782	Venus 176	1196	Venus 188	2613	Felsa 4002
783	Venus 179	1197	Venus 188	2907	FHF 28
785	Venus 191	1198	Venus 188	2931	Felsa 4010
786	Venus 178	1199	Venus 188	2932	Felsa 4010
787	Venus 152	1577	Valjoux 320	2933	Felsa 4010
788	Venus 152	1577	Valjoux 320	2935	Felsa 4010
789	Venus 151	1765	Venus 178	2936	Felsa 4010
790	Venus 150	1806	Breitling 11/12	3306	Felsa 4010
791	Venus 185	1808	Breitling 11/12	3307	Felsa 4010
796	Venus 176	1809	Breitling 11/12/14	3865	ETA 2472
799	Venus 187	2000	Venus 188	4003	Felsa 4012
800	Venus 190	2002	Venus 188	4008	Felsa 4014
801	Venus 190	2003	Valjoux 7730	4009	Felsa 4014
803	Valjoux VZHC	2004	Valjoux 7730/7733	4010	Felsa 4012
804	Valjoux VZHCL	2005	Venus 188	4515	Peseux 330
805	Valjoux VZHCL	2005	Valjoux 7731	4515	Peseux 330
806	Venus 178	2006	Valjoux 7730	4516	Peseux 330
807	Venus 150	2008	Valjoux 7730/7733	4517	Peseux 330
808	Valjoux 7735	2009/CR	Venus 188	5037	FHF 75
809	Venus 178	2009	Valjoux 7730/7733	5201	AS 2063
810	Venus 178	2010	Valjoux 7730/7733	5215	FEF 430
810 24H	Venus 178	2016	Valjoux 7730	5216	FEF 430
811	Valjoux 236	2030	Valjoux 7734	5217	FEF 430
812	Valjoux 724	2110	Breitling 12	5218	FEF 430
814	Valjoux 7738	2111	Breitling 15	5219	FEF 430
815	Valjoux 7736	2111	Breitling 15		

Ref.No.	Caliber	Ref.No.	Caliber	Series No.	Year Made
5591	AS 1012	80191	BREITLING 233	563659-568959	1944
5592	AS 1012	80250	ETA 2892-2	568971-636507	1945
5593	AS 1012	80260	ETA 956.112	636508-692266	1946
5594	AS 1012	80290	ETA 2892-2	703562-717737	1947
5595	AS 1012	80350	Piguet 1270	717784-728688	1948
5596	ETA 2410	80360	ETA 988.332	728724-740210	1949
5597	ETA 2410	80510	ETA 955.412	740405-769843	1950
5598	ETA 2410	80560	ETA 956.112	769844-808456	1951
5599	ETA 2410	80770	BREITLING 300-1	808457-817915	1952
5600	AS 1012	80792	BREITLING 233	817916-832126	1953
5601	ETA 2410	80975	BREITLING 232	832127-844123	1954
5602	ETA 2410	81500	Ronda 732	844124-868778	1955
5603	AS 1012	81600	Lemania 1873-24H	868779-889562	1956
5604	AS 1012	81610	Valjoux 7750	889563-898029	1957
5606	AS 1012	81950	Valjoux 7750	898830-910504	1958
5607	AS 1012	81970	ETA 2892-2	910505-922163	1959
5624	AS 1012	81980	BREITLING	922164-933063	1960
			7000-ETA 2892-2	933064-947803	1961
5626	AS 1012	89520	Lemanic 1873	947804-963553	1962
5629	AS 1012			963554-975997	1963
5630	AS 1012			975998-1002734	1964
5631	AS 1012			1002735-1060398	1965
5632	AS 1012			1060399-1122809	1966
5634	Peseux 340			1122810-1204581	1967
5635	Peseux 340			1204582-1262904	1968
5636	Peseux 340			1262905-1337825	1969
5637	Peseux 340			1337826-1356899	1970
5638	Peseux 340			1356900-1382203	1971
5639	Peseux 340			1382204-1406566	1972
5640	Peseux 340			1406567-1426969	1973
5641	Peseux 340			1426970-1433372	1974
5642	Peseux 340			1433373-1439417	1975
5643	Peseux 340			1439418-1442922	1976
5644	Peseux 340			1442923-1448464	1977
5645	Peseux 340			1448465-1448473	1978
6764	Felsa 4062				
7104	Valjoux 7740				
7105	FHF 57				
7106	FHF 57				
7107	ETA 2360				
7108	ETA 2360				
7656	Valjoux 7736				
7660	Venus 178				
7662	Breitling 12				
7806	Valjoux 7740				
8506	AS 1193				
8506	Breitling 12				
80180	ETA 955.412				

Chronology of the Breitling Firm

1884 Breitling firm founded in St. Imier by Leon Breitling

1892 Firm moved to La Chaux-de-Fonds and renamed Leon G. Breitling S.A. Montbrillant Watch Manufactory

1914 Death of Leon Breitling; firm taken over by Gaston Breitling

1915 Breitling markets a stopwatch that can be worn on the arm

1927 Death of Gaston Breitling

1932 Firm taken over by Willy Breitling

1934 Breitling markets the first chronograph with two buttons

1936 Chronograph for use on aircraft marketed

1939 Large contract for chronographs from Royal Air Force

1942 Chronomat first marketed

1947 Breitling Watch Company of America enters stock exchange in New York

1952 Navitimer first marketed

1956 Breitling has great success in the USA

1958 Super Ocean series first marketed

1962 Breitling introduces the Cosmonaute

1963 Top Time series first marketed

1966 Tremendous popularity of chronographs; many varieties offered by Breitling

1967 Chronoslide sales influence the industry

1969 Automatic chronograph first marketed

1972 Breitling offers its greatest variety of chronographs

1975 Breitling markets the quartz-powered chronograph

1976 Automatic Chronomat in new case first marketed

1977 Autotimer and LED version of Navitimer marketed

1978 LCD version of Navitimer marketed

1979 Death of Willy Breitling, factory closed, trade name bought by Ernest Schneider, production begins in a new factory in Grenchen

1980 Pluto, Jupiter, and Mars chronographs first marketed

1981 New watch series introduced in collaboration with Eric Tabarly

1982 GMT watch first marketed

1983 Deep Sea watch for depths to 1000 meters, with safety valve, first marketed

1984 Breitling centennial; new version of the old Chronomat marketed

1985 Compass model (watch with compass) marketed by Breitling

1986 New version of legendary Navitimer marketed

1987 Breitling markets watch series in collaboration with the Ellesse firm

1988 Breitling markets the World watch with four time zones

1990 Duograph, with second time zone, and Astromat marketed

1991 Astromat series introduced by Breitling

1992 Breitling introduces world's smallest chronograph and Navitimer 92

1993 Breitling introduces Navitimer Rattapante and Navitimer QP with perpetual calendar

1994 The Chronomat series, revised in 1984 (first type offered in 1942) celebrates its tenth anniversary

Closing Comments

There is probably a lot more that should be put into this book! Yet despite this, one has to stop somewhere. As an old German saying goes: "When one comes from city hall, one is always smarter." In a sense, this saying could well apply here too. All the informative material that has been assembled was examined and organized, and as soon as it was finalized new material arrived, creating the necessity to re-organize everything. More and more editing became necessary, leading to what at times seemed like an endless task. And yet. . . .

What was said at the beginning of this book about its completeness is true: documenting all examples is impossible, and yet I believe that so much has been brought together here about the history of the Breitling firm that we can almost proclaim that a certain completeness has been achieved. The major milestones of the firm's history have been told, a well-rounded picture has surely resulted.

I would like to express my hearty thanks for the support that I have received from many collectors, their interesting conversations and the helpful information and encouragement that followed from it. My special thanks go to the firm of Trautmann Uhren and Mr. Trautmann, Sr., who had collaborated with Breitling since 1947 and who gave me a great deal of help. I would also like to extend very hearty thanks to Mrs. B. Breitling. Frau Breitling made old photos and business documents available, which added considerably to completing the story of the Breitling firm. Thanks also go to the firm of Breitling in Grenchen, which made technical information available to me. Also, a few holes were filled by the Auktionshaus Joseph of Mr. G. Joseph, with their catalogues. Further thanks go to Mr. C. Pfeiffer-Belli and Mrs. Andrea Hölzl of Callwey Publishers for examining the manuscript. Mr. Pfeiffer-Belli himself, the author of several books about watches, gave me much appreciated encouraging advice

and support. Likewise I would like to thank Mr. G. R. Lang, and very great thanks go to Mr. G. Gaspari, without whose help it would have been impossible to include many minute details.

The majority of the watches shown in this book are from the author's collection or from the Breitling firm. Several collectors also allowed me to photograph their fine examples, and others have given me their finest photos. I would like to heartily acknowledge everyone else's help here, even though most have asked me not to mention them by name.

If any readers have any further information and details about the Breitling firm, I would like them to contact me through the publisher. Perhaps a subsequent new edition would make the history of Breitling even more complete.

Bibliography

1. Catalogs of the Breitling firm from 1900 to 1993.
2. Gisbert L. Brunner, Armbanduhren, Munich, 1990.
3. A, Kreuzer, Die Uhr am Handgelenk, Klagenfurt, 1982.
4. Die Chronomatik, reprint from the "Neue Züricher Zeitung", technical section, December 1969, from Hans Kocher, Biel.
5. Chrono-Matic, Automatischer Chronograph, technical guide from the Breitling firm, Sept. 1970.
6. Gisbert L. Brunner & Christian Pfeiffer-Belli, Schweizer Armbanduhren, Munich, 1990.
7. L'Information Horlogêre Suisse, La Chaux-de-Fonds, 1979.
8. G. Nigretti & F. Nencini, Die schönsten Armbanduhren vergangener Jahrzehnte, Munich, 1986.
9. G. Schindler, Uhren, Munich, 1975.
10. Kahlert, Mühe & Brunner, Armbanduhren, 100 - jährige Entwicklungsgeschichte, Munich, 1983.
11. M. Rehor, Mechanische Uhren, Berlin, 1986.
12. G. L. Brunner, Armbanduhren mit Weltzeitindikation, article from "Alte Uhren" No. 4/90, pp. 33-39.

Index

The numbers refer to pages in the text except for those preceded by *, which refer to illustrations. Watch types are cited in quotation marks.

Photo Credits

Auktionen Joseph, Mönchengladbach: 16, 17, 24-25, 28-32, 59-60

Author: 18-23, 27, 34, 40-48, 62-68, 72, 75-79, 87-88, 91, 93-96, 101, 102, 104, 106, 109-112, 115-116, 118, 128, 146, 147, 149, 150

Breitling, B., Cortova: 11, 13-15, 33, 36, 38, 39, 69, 99, 100, 147, 148

Breitling firm, Grenchen: 54, 55, 108, 113, 129-136, 138-142, 143 above

Callwey Verlag, Munich: 18, 56, 104

G. Caspari, Geneva: 35, 37, 50, 51, 71, 74, 80, 83, 84, 86, 90, 119, 137

Hartmann, Cologne: 103, 104

Lang, G. R., Munich: 2, 4, 12, 58, 61, 62, 92, 120 123

Trautmann firm, Karlsruhe: 53, 70, 73, 81, 82, 85, 105, 107, 143 below, 144, 145

OTHER SCHIFFER TITLES

www.schifferbooks.com

Swiss Wristwatches, Chronology of Worldwide Success Gisbert Brunner & Christian Pfeiffer-Belli. An overview of Swiss wristwatch designs in the 20th century with nearly 650 photo illustrations. The many forms and styles of casings, dials, and hands are covered, along with manufacturers' literature, advertising, and catalogs. The firms of Omega, Longines, Tavannes-Cyma, Breitling, Doxa, Universal, Movado, and Zenith are represented, and a price guide makes it a valuable reference for collectors of wristwatches.

Size: 9" x 12"	648 illus.	248 pp.
Price Guide		
ISBN: 0-88740-301-8	hard cover	$69.95

Automatic Wristwatches from Germany, England, France, Japan, Russia and the USA Heinz Hampel. While often associated with Switzerland, manufacturers in many other nations have produced wonderful automatic wristwatches. Richly illustrated with over 400 photos the work of German, English, French, Japanese, Russian and the US watchmakers is explored. A total of 123 watches are illustrated in three different views and are described in detail. A price guide is provided for collectors.

Size: 9" x 12"	400 photos	216 pp.
Value Guide\Index		
ISBN: 0-7643-0379-1	hard cover	$79.95

Automatic Wristwatches from Switzerland, Watches that Wind Themselves Heinz Hampel. The automatic mechanism was a major advance in the history of the wristwatch. The successful design became the hallmark of the skilled Swiss watchmaker as the technology developed in the years from 1926 to 1978. 200 watches are discussed representing all the Swiss manufacturers. Each is illustrated with three photos to show the dial, and the complete and partly disassembled movement. Information on their mechanism and construction is offered along with data needed to locate the watches chronologically and a current price guide.

Size: 9" x 12"	500+ photos	352 pp.
Price Guide		
ISBN: 0-88740-609-2	hard cover	$79.95

Rolex Wristwatches, An Unauthorized History James M. Dowling & Jeffrey P. Hess. Nearly 400 color photographs celebrate the watches produced by Rolex over the last 90 years. Lavishly illustrated with color photographs that capture their beauty and technological innovation, this is the most thorough and extensive history of the company ever written. Information for collectors is also provided, including a current price guide.

Size: 9" x 12"	392 photos	320 pp.
Price Guide		
ISBN: 0-7643-0011-3	hard cover	$125.00

Wristwatch Chronometers, Mechanical Precision Watches and Their Testing Fritz von Osterhausen. A richly illustrated, detailed account of wristwatch chronometers and the rigorous testing they must undergo to become certified. Over 400 photos document this crowning achievement of the watchmakers art while information about testing methods, procedures, and guidelines make it clear how great a challenge it has been. A compilation of participating makers based on Swiss Testing Agencies' yearly reports from 1925 and the Swiss Observatories' reports is included as is a guide to current values.

Size: 9" x 12"	414 photos	214 pp.
Price Guide		
ISBN: 0-7643-0375-9	hard cover	$79.95

Chronograph Wristwatches, To Stop Time Gerd-R. Lang & Reinhard Meis. Hundreds of photographs illustrate this outstanding look at the history, development, and identification of wrist chronographs—mechanical wristwatches that, in addition to their normal clockwork, have a mechanism that allows them to time short-term events. Both the technological and design achievements are explored and celebrated. A price guide is included for collectors.

Size: 9" x 12"	675+ photos & illus.	256 pp.
Price Guide		
ISBN: 0-88740-502-9	hard cover	$79.95

Wristwatches, History of a Century's Development *Revised and Expanded 4th Edition* Helmut Kahlert, Richard Muhë, and Gisbert L. Brunner. This respected reference for collectors of wristwatches includes hundreds of watches in nearly 2000 photos, which celebrate both the style and mechanics of the designs. Watches from around the world, their makers, technological changes, construction, and automatic features all are discussed. A current price guide by noted authority Gordon Converse is included.

Size: 9" x 12"	1994 photos & illus.	410 pp.
Revised Price Guide		
ISBN: 0-7643-0861-0	hard cover	$79.95

Omega Designs, Feast for the Eyes Anton Kreuzer. An illustrated description of all the watch movements manufactured by the Omega Watch Co. since the registration of its trademark in 1894. Over 400 watches are shown in 414 photographs. The company has made precision pocket- and wristwatches including the world famous chronometer wristwatch Constellation, the diver's watch Seamaster, and the chronograph wristwatch Speedmaster Professional. Collectors will value the information and the current price guide.

Size: 8 1/2" x 11"	414 photos	224 pp.
Price Guide		
ISBN: 0-7643-0058-X	hard cover	$59.95

The Movado History Fritz von Osterhausen. A lavishly illustrated history of Movado from its roots in the Jura Mountains in 1881 through more than a century of tradition and technological advancement. Over the years, Movado earned a reputation for pioneering the art of wristwatches, high-precision movements, and watches with complications, as well as water-resistant watches, and their accomplishments are celebrated here in 250 color photos and informative text.
Size: 8 1/2" x 11"   250 color photos   234 pp.
Index
ISBN: 0-7643-0126-8   hard cover $89.95

Time in Gold Wristwatches Gerald Viola & Gisbert L. Brunner. The history of the 18 leading luxury wristwatch companies of Switzerland richly illustrated with beautiful photos. Here are the most important and elegant watches of Audemars Piguet, Baume & Mercier, Blancpain, Breguet, Cartier, Chopad, Corum, Ebel, Gerald Genta, Gerard-Perregaux, IWC, Jaeger-LeCoultre, Patek Philippe, Piaget, Rolex, Ulysse Nardin, Vacheron Constantin, and Technisches Kapitel, making this an indispensible reference for collectors and historians.
Size: 9" x 12"   450 photos   256 pp.
ISBN: 0-88740-137-6   hard cover $79.95

Comic Character Timepieces, Seven Decades of Memories Hy Brown with Nancy Thomas. This delightful book covers the lighter side of horological history. Comic character timepieces from the earliest clocks to the present day quartz wristwatches have delighted children and adults alike, with some of the more creative or popular ones being avidly sought after by collectors. With hundreds of beautiful color photos, this is a celebration of American imagination and artistry. A price guide completes the work.
Size: 9" x 12"   786 color photos   280 pp.
Value Guide
ISBN: 0-88740-426-X   hard cover $79.95

Marine and Pocket Chronometers Hans von Bertele. The development of the chronometer was an important step in the development of the navigational arts. Nearly 350 of these handsome, complicated timepieces are illustrated here with a special emphasis on their movements. The book follows the history of the chronometer, with short biographies of the most important manufacturers and an extensive appendix.
Size: 9" x 12"   9 color and 269 b/w photos   216 pp.
ISBN: 0-88740-303-4   hard cover $135.00

American Shelf and Wall Clocks, A Pictorial History for Collectors *Revised & Expanded 2nd Edition* Robert W.D. Ball. Over 1250 American shelf and wall clocks in a variety of forms and designs are each beautifully illustrated and accompanied by an informative text. This historical overview covers the centuries and is an important guide. The up-to-date price guide is useful.
Size: 9" x 12"   1250+ clocks   272 pp.
Revised Price Guide
ISBN: 0-7643-0905-6   hard cover $69.95

British Longcase Clocks Derek Roberts. The longcase clock has a special place in horological history. Here, illustrated with over 300 photos, is valuable information detailing its British origin and evolution, and the range of longcase clocks produced since the sixteenth century. Included are clocks of the Victorian, Edwardian, and modern times. A glossary of terms and index of makers complete this important reference.
Size: 9" x 12"   over 300 photos   400 pp.
Index
ISBN: 0-88740-230-5   hard cover $95.00

European Pendulum Clocks Klaus Maurice & Peter Heuer. Nearly 450 beautiful photos illustrate pendulum clocks from France, England, Holland, Scandinavia, and the German-speaking countries. Wall, cabinet, and free-standing styles are included, accompanied by full explanations of each clock in this authoritative study.
Size: 8 1/2" x 11"   448 photos   248 pp.
Index
ISBN: 0-88740-144-9   hard cover $59.95

Chester County Clocks and Their Makers *Second Edition* Arthur E. James. The early clockmakers of Chester County, Pennsylvania gave the traditional designs of the era a unique and beautiful regional interpretation. This classic work explores the clocks and their makers, preserving their heritage for the ages.
Size: 5 1/2" x 8 1/2"   76 b/w photos & 77 drawings   222 pp.
ISBN: 0-916838-04-8   hard cover $20.00

Continental and American Skeleton Clocks Derek Roberts. Instead of hiding the mechanical workings of the clock, skeleton clocks celebrated them, leaving them visible for all to marvel at. The style attracted the attention of some of the finest clockmakers, particularly those working in France from circa 1760–1860. Here is a beautifully illustrated exploration of these fascinating clocks from European and American makers.
Size: 9" x 12"   249 illustrations   288 pp.
Index
ISBN: 0-88740-182-1   hard cover $79.95

Carriage and Other Traveling Clocks Derek Roberts. Nearly seven hundred traveling clocks illustrated with beautiful photos are accompanied by explanations of all the major designers' work in this form, beginning from the 17th century. Special chapters present the work of noted clockmakers. The book displays these fantastically stunning works of art and more common popular styles available today.
Size: 9" x 12"   685+ photos   368 pp.
Index
ISBN: 0-88740-454-5   hard cover $99.95

Black Forest Clocks Rick Ortenburger. Over 600 Black Forest clocks are illustrated in this important horological study. Many wonderful cuckoo and singing bird clocks, early glass bell, trumpeter, Jockele, animation, and picture frame clocks all have been made in this region of Germany, where a growing number of skilled clockmakers have practiced their art for 300 years. This book, with its guide to current prices, has been welcomed by collectors around the world.
Size: 8 1/2" x 11"   600+ Black Forest Clocks   300 pp.
Price Guide
ISBN: 0-88740-300-X   hard cover $79.95

Vienna Regulator Clocks Rick Ortenburger. Since their introduction around 1780, Vienna Regulator clocks became a familiar style in homes and public spaces around Europe and the world. Produced in Vienna, Austria, the forms have moved from their early and transitional designs to serpentine, altdeutsch, Baroque, and factory-made types with one, two-, and three-weight movements. In continuous production until the 1930s, they continue to be popular with collectors and decorators today. A value guide is included.
Size: 8 1/2" x 11"   348 photos   180 pp.
Value Guide/Index
ISBN: 0-88740-224-0   hard cover $39.95

Advertising Clocks, America's Timeless Heritage Michael Bruner. From wooden mechanical clocks of the 1870s to later neon electric models, American advertising clocks are celebrated in many diverse styles to promote any product: beverages, cigarettes, manufacturers, Over 300 are described and illustrated with color photos.

Size: 8 1/2" x 11"	300 color photos	128 pp.

Price Guide
ISBN: 0-88740-790-0 soft cover $29.95

French Bronze Clocks, 1700-1830 Elke Niehüser. Beautiful gold and bronze pendulum clocks not only tell time but also depict sculptures of Greek and Roman mythology, American Indians, and African figures. The symbolism of the figures is explained to reflect nearly-lost allegories that were well known 150 years ago. Over 200 color and many black and white photos display these fabulous clocks. An important additional feature is a visual directory of 1365 bronze clocks with bibliographic references that will hertofore make researching the field much more efficient.

Size: 9" x 12" 211 color & 1456 b/w photos 272 pp.
ISBN: 0-7643-0943-9 hard cover $89.95

Mystery, Novelty, & Fantasy Clocks Derek Roberts. Over 300 clocks, for buildings or tabletops, which do far more than tell time, are presented with concise historical explanations, detailed drawings, and clear color photography. 700 years of clocks are studied, clocks that display magical acts, appear to require no power to drive them, or have no apparent connection between the movement and the hands. These mystery clocks are fascinating mechanisms.

Size: 9" x 12" 330 color, 176 b/w photos 288 pp.
ISBN: 0-7643-0873-4 hard cover $150

The Incredible Ball Point Pen, A Comprehensive History & Price Guide Henry Gostony & Stuart Schneider. A celebration of the revolutionary ball point pen, illustrated with more than 450 color photos. Collectors and historians will be fascinated with its painful development and its roll-coaster ride to the public and technological success that followed. Today its reliability and and universal acceptance makes it the standard writing instrument around the world. The ball point pen has taken hundreds of forms over the years making it a natural for collectors. A price guide completes this wonderful book.

Size: 8 1/2" x 11" 469 color photos 160 pp.
Price Guide/Index
ISBN: 0-7643-0437-2 soft cover $29.95

Fountain Pens and Pencils, The Golden Age of Writing Instruments Revised 2nd Edition George Fischler & Stuart Schneider. The 2nd edition of the premier study of fountain pens and pencils. Over 1000 fountain pens are illustrated in full color, life- or near life-sized photographs. Extensively researched, it chronicles the history of fountain pens, the companies that made them, and the many innovations that made them practical in everyday use. Current prices are included for the collector.

Size: 9" x 12" 970 color photos 320 pp.
Revised Price Guide
ISBN: 0-7643-0491-7 hard cover $89.95

Victorian Pencils, Tools to Jewels Deb Crosby. A groundbreaking study of the development of mechanical and metal cased pencils in the nineteenth century. Illustrated with over 700 photographs, the book provides examples of the extraordinary variety of propelling pencils that were created between 1800 and 1920. Readers will be struck by the ingenuity of the inventors and creators of this (until now) forgotten form of decorative art. Includes value ranges.

Size: 8 1/2" x 11" 706 color photos 224 pp.
Price Guide/Index
ISBN: 0-7643-0413-5 hard cover $59.95

The Illustrated Guide to Antique Writing Instruments *Revised and Expanded 3rd Edition* Stuart Schneider & George Fischler. A quick and easy reference for pen and pencil collectors. Over 500 pens and pencils in beautiful, nearly full-size color photos. Short histories of the 19 main companies are provided. Concise, helpful information with each photo includes a guide to the current price of each.

Size: 6" x 9" 556 color photos 160 pp.
Revised Price Guide
ISBN: 0-7643-0980-3 soft cover $19.95

Collecting Writing Instruments Dietmar Geyer. From the flint tool to the stylus, from quill pen to fountain pen to felt-tip marker, this book invites readers to develop or deepen their love for beautiful old writing instruments. Contains hundreds of contemporary engravings, illustrations, advertisements, photos, and catalog and brochure excerpts.

Size: 9" x 12" Hundreds of illustrations 176 pp.
Price Guide
ISBN: 0-88740-272-0 hard cover $49.95

Canes, From the Seventeenth to the Twentieth Century Jeffrey B. Snyder. A magnificent tour of canes and staffs, ranging from folk art to formal designs, depicted in 900 color photos. Here are rare and common canes, canes with handles bearing human and animal forms, scrimshaw, glass, gadget, weapon, political, and presentation canes. Cane terminology, dating techniques, and formal cane etiquette are also discussed. There is also an availability guide to help the collector assess the rarity of a cane and its effect of value.

Size: 9" x 12" 900 color photos 288 pp.
Availability Guide
ISBN: 0-88740-549-5 hard cover $69.95

Walkingsticks Ulrich Klever. A comprehensive look at decorative walking sticks, including their use, history, and craftsmanship. A chapter on materials familiarizes the reader with the wide range of canes available. This cultural and commercial history will become a useful reference for historians as well as dealers and collectors. A price guide is included.

Size: 8 1/2" x 11" 285+ photos & illus. 244 pp.
Price Guide
ISBN: 0-7643-0154-3 soft cover $29.95

US $49.95

9 780764 326707
5 4995

ISBN: 978-0-7643-2670-7